FUNDAMENTALS OF
ENGLISH GRAMMAR:
AN ECLECTIC APPROACH

Gideon Olushola Dada

Fundamentals of English Grammar: An Eclectic Approach

Copyright © 2021 by Gideon Olushola Dada

Department of English

Federal College of Education

Pankshin, Plateau State, Nigeria

gideonolusholadada@gmail.com

+2348036798439 or +2348051278783

First published in 2021 by:

Olabooks International

Washington, DC 20032, USA

http://www.olabooksinternationalselfpub.com

olabooksinternational@gmail.com

ISBN: 978-1-7353-6716-3

All rights reserved. No part of this book may be reprinted, reproduced or utilized in any form or by any electronic, mechanical, or other means, now known or hereafter invented, including photocopying and recording or in any information storage or retrieval system, without prior permission in writing from the copyright owner.

Printed in the United States of America

OLABOOKS INTERNATIONAL
MY BOOK • MY PASSION

REVIEWERS' THOUGHTS ON THE BOOK

Fundamentals of English Grammar: An Eclectic Approach is a text every student and teacher of English should have and consult regularly. It contains the essentials of English grammar, from the morpheme to the largest possible grammatical construction, with a guide on English grammar in use. The most striking feature of this text in my opinion is the simplicity with which the author presents the complexities and technicalities that characterize English grammar.

Andrew Onoja, *Department of English, University of Jos*

The author has carefully and beautifully made the study of English grammar easy for all second language learners of English with the learner-friendly approach to the issues addressed in the text. I therefore strongly recommend the text for all students in Nigerian tertiary institutions, and for anyone interested in English language studies.

Innocent N. Dajang, *Department of English, University of Jos*

The author has done a great job. The book is simplified, very rich and I have learnt a great deal from it. It is suitable for both colleges and higher institutions of learning.

Adesewa O. Olatunde (Mrs), *Department of Languages, Federal Polytechnic, Bida*

Fundamentals of English Grammar: An Eclectic Approach is a comprehensive companion for students who aspire to study English beyond the intermediate level.

Thomas Abah, *Department of English, Federal College of Education, Pankshin*

Fundamentals of English Grammar: An Eclectic Approach undertakes the task of making contemporary grammar accessible to learners. The author adopts a straight-to-the-point approach in his definition of concepts, coupled with robust illustrations of each topic. He should be commended for the array of selected topics, as these cover the major aspects of English grammar for tertiary students of English.

Gbenga Joseph, *Department of English, Federal College of Education, Pankshin*

CONTENTS

DEDICATION xii

ACKNOWLEDGEMENTS xiii

FOREWORD xvi

PREFACE xix

Chapter One: **INTRODUCTION** 1

    1.1 The Concept of Grammar 1

    1.2 Theories of Grammar 3

    1.2.1 Traditional Grammar 3

    1.2.2 Structural Grammar 3

    1.2.3 Transformational Generative Grammar 4

    1.2.4 Systemic Functional Grammar 4

    1.3 Grammatical Continuum 5

    1.4 Grammar and Syntax 6

    1.5 Eclecticism as Applicable to this Book 7

PART ONE: MORPHOLOGY 9

Chapter Two: THE MORPHEME 10

2.1 The Morpheme and Morphology 10

2.2 Types of Morpheme 11

2.2.1 Free Morphemes 12

2.2.2 Bound Morphemes 12

2.3 Morphological Processes in English 16

2.4 Segmentability of Morphemes 21

2.5 Other Terminology in Morphology 21

Chapter Three: THE WORD: THE OPEN CLASS 27

3.1 Word Classes in English 27

3.2 The Open Class 28

3.2.1 Nouns 28

3.2.2 Adjectives 43

3.2.3 Verbs 53

3.2.4 Adverbs 88

Chapter Four: THE WORD: THE CLOSED CLASS 95

4.1 The Closed Class 95

4.1.1 Pronouns 96

4.1.2 Prepositions 105

4.1.3 Conjunctions 112

4.1.4 Interjections 118

4.1.5 Determiners 120

4.2 The Multifunctionality of English Words 127

PART TWO: SYNTAX 131

Chapter Five: **THE PHRASE 132**

5.1 The Concept of Phrase 132

5.2 Types of Phrases 133

5.2.1 Noun Phrases 133

5.2.2 Adjectival Phrases 135

5.2.3 Verb Phrases 137

5.2.4 Adverbial Phrases 140

5.2.5 Prepositional Phrases 144

5.2.6 Appositive Phrases 146

5.2.7 Gerundial Phrases 147

5.2.8 Infinitival Phrases 148

5.2.9 Participial Phrases 149

5.2.10 Determiner Phrases: A Proposition 151

Chapter Six: **THE CLAUSE 156**

6.1 The Meaning of Clause 156

6.2 The Structure of the Clause 156

6.3 Types of Clause 158

6.3.1 Independent Clause 158

6.3.2 Dependent Clause 158

Chapter Seven: THE SENTENCE 170

7.1 Sentence Defined 170

7.2 The Structure of the Sentence 171

7.3 Classification of Sentences 171

7.3.1 Classification of Sentences Based on Function 171

7.3.2 Classification of Sentences Based on Structure 172

7.3.3 Classification of Sentences Based on Size 175

7.4 The Structure of Simple Sentences 177

7.5 Tree Diagrams in Syntax 179

7.6 Grammar and Context 183

PART THREE: ENGLISH GRAMMAR IN USE 185

Chapter Eight: APPLICATION OF SYNTACTIC RULES 186

8.1 Active Voice and Passive Voice 186

8.2 Question Tags 188

8.2.1 Rules for Question Tags 189

8.2.2 The Structure of Question Tags 189

8.3 Direct Speech and Indirect Speech 193

8.3.1 Use of Tenses 193

8.3.2 Use of Pronouns 194

8.3.3 Use of Determiners 195

8.3.4 Use of Words Denoting Distance and Time 195

8.3.5 Indirect Speech and the Sentence Types 196

8.4 Conditional Sentences 198

8.4.1 First Conditionals/Open Conditions/Real Conditions 199

8.4.2 Second Conditionals/Closed Conditions/Unreal Conditions 200

8.4.3 Third Conditionals/Unfulfilled Conditions 200

8.5 Concord in English 201

8.5.1 Subject-Verb Concord 202

8.5.2 Subject-Complement Concord 208

8.5.3 Subject-Object Concord 209

8.5.4 Pronoun-Antecedent Concord 209

8.5.5 Determiner-Antecedent Concord 209

Chapter Nine: **COMMON ERRORS IN ENGLISH GRAMMAR 213**

9.1 Error or Mistake? 213

9.2 Morphological Errors 213

9.2.1 Errors Relating to the Use of Nouns 214

9.2.2 Errors Relating to the Use of Adjectives 216

9.2.3 Errors Relating to the Use of Verbs 217

9.2.4 Errors Relating to the Use of Adverbs 219

9.2.5 Errors Relating to the Use of Pronouns 221

9.2.6 Errors Relating to the Use of Prepositions 223

9.2.7 Errors Relating to the Use of Conjunctions 225

9.2.8 Errors Relating to the Use of Determiners 227

9.3 Syntactic Errors 229

9.3.1 Sentence Logic Error 229

9.3.2 Faulty Subordination 230

9.3.3 Excessive Subordination 230

9.3.4 Faulty Parallelism 231

9.3.5 Concord Error 232

9.3.6 Vague Pronoun Reference 232

9.3.7 Dangling Modifiers 233

9.3.8 Sentence Fragments 234

9.3.9 Run-on Sentences and Comma Splices 234

9.3.10 Inconsistent Tenses 235

Chapter Ten: APPENDIX: THE MECHANICS OF WRITING 238

10.1 Capitalization 238

10.2 Punctuation 239

10.3 Spelling 246

REFERENCES 252

DEDICATION

To my dear mother, late **Mrs Felicia Ayoka Dada** (10th March, 1945 to 11th June, 2020) who, with my father, struggled against all odds to educate me up to university level.

ACKNOWLEDGEMENTS

First of all, I am grateful to the Almighty God for His gracious gifts of wisdom, knowledge, understanding and strength to undertake the task of writing this book.

I deeply appreciate my former lecturer, Professor Sola Timothy Babatunde (National President, English Scholars' Association of Nigeria), for accepting to write the foreword to the book, in spite of his very busy schedule. Thank you, sir, for being a mentor par excellence and a father extraordinaire. Thank you, also, for having confidence in me, always.

I am indebted to the following friends for meticulously editing the initial drafts of the book and offering suggestions that helped to improve it. They are Andrew Onoja, Innocent Dajang (both of the Department of English, University of Jos, Jos), Mrs Adesewa Olatunde (of the Department of Languages, Federal Polytechnic, Bida), Thomas Abah and Gbenga Joseph (both of English Department, Federal College of Education, Pankshin). I should note, however, that we are not agreed on every issue raised. Therefore, the final opinions expressed in the book are mine and any surviving imperfections in it are, regrettably, my sole responsibility.

Over the years, in my academic voyage, many teachers, too numerous to mention, have contributed to my success but I will not fail to acknowledge the following for their outstanding contributions to my knowledge of the English language in general and English grammar in particular. First, Mr Dele Ogunniyi of Oyun Baptist High School, Ijagbo, Kwara State, laid the solid foundation for my knowledge of English. Dr J.A.

Duntoye of Kwara State College of Education, Ilorin, ignited my passion for English grammar in its morpho-syntactic sense. Professor Mahfouz Adedimeji of the University of Ilorin, Ilorin, nurtured and sustained my interest in this area of English study by introducing me to Systemic Functional Grammar while Professor Sola Timothy Babatunde, also of the University of Ilorin, at both undergraduate and postgraduate levels, consolidated the knowledge with Transformational Generative Grammar. I am immeasurably indebted to you all.

I am grateful to all my colleagues in the Department of English, Federal College of Education, Pankshin, for the brotherly warmth and camaraderie that exist among us and for the privilege of cross-fertilization of ideas that indirectly birthed this book. I may not mention names because of obvious constraints but I do appreciate you all.

Also, I thank all my students whom I taught the contents of this book. Since I informed them of writing it some years ago, many of them did not relent in asking about its progress. Their persistent asking nudged me on, even when the going was tough. Similarly, in August, 2020, I started *English Grammar Online* series (based on Chapter Nine of this book), through which I taught a host of virtual students on Facebook. I wish to appreciate the following people: Dr Olatunde Odewumi, Bizuum Yadok (for scholarly contributions to the topics discussed), Sammy Best, Shola Ajani Ibiwoye and Barr. Dare Komolafe (for encouragement in various ways).

The managements and staffs of Olabooks International, Washington DC, United States of America and Rex Productions, Jos, Nigeria did a good job on the publishing and printing of the book respectively. I am grateful to them.

Finally, I wish to thank my wife, Opeyemi, for her unquantifiable support and sacrifice, continuous encouragement and passionate concern about the timely completion of the book. Our children: Oluwadara, Oluwadamilola and Ife-Oluwa also deserve a mention for putting up with my inadequacies in the course of writing the book.

FOREWORD

The teaching of various aspects of the Grammar of English continues to be a major hurdle for all teachers of the English language, especially in the tertiary institutions in Nigeria where English functions as a Second Language (ESL). The English language is called upon to perform heavy communicative functions in this context, such that a student of English is expected to know the language and know about it. It is more serious if such a student is being trained to train others in the use of English in Nigeria. In the situation being described, Grammar, which is the scientific study of the rules of a language, is central.

The English language is known to be rule-governed but at the same time arbitrary because of the numerous inconsistencies in the application of the rules. It can thus be said that the language has numerous linguistic problems which constantly constitute major impediments to its effective learning and use. Taking pains to carefully study, learn and teach the grammar of English is always a very rewarding task.

Over the years, some of the following functions of grammar have been agreed upon in the literature:

Grammar is the study of language. Grammar thus illuminates the linguistic problems inherent in the language at the levels of syntax, phonology and lexico-semantics; and it suggests ways of overcoming those problems so as to use the language effectively.

Grammar studies words, their formation and their classification into various categories. It also progresses to help us see the various categories in a systematic way by grouping them into the various parts of speech. In this way, grammar demonstrates the interrelationships among the classes of words e.g. the Open and Closed Systems.

The study of sentence structure and patterns is central to grammar. Grammar gives information on how words, which are smaller units, are combined to form larger units. It reveals what can be combined, how they are combined and the outcome of the patterns created by these combinations. It is not enough to know about the patterns, it is crucial that we know how the patterns can be used for effective communication.

A major aspect of language use for communication is writing. Writing is indeed the most complex and most demanding of the four language skills of listening, speaking, reading and writing. Grammar is an asset for anyone who desires to be a successful writer. The training in paragraph writing for different kinds of essays exposes the learner to the different lexical and grammatical devices for achieving textual cohesion; and for manipulating the language for elegant and dignified style in written communication. Knowledge of grammar enhances a writer's ability to create text and interact effectively with the audience.

We can thus see that it is impossible to be empowered for effective communication without focused instruction in the grammar of a language – more so if the language is a second language.

The book, *Fundamentals of English Grammar: An Eclectic Approach,* by Gideon Olushola Dada thus provides users of English in the Outer Circle what is needed for effective communication in the language. The book has incorporated all the functions of grammar mentioned above into its fabric in a perfect mix – the hallmark of an accomplished chef.

A major quality of this book however is its Applied Linguistic (AL) approach. AL is problem-driven, not theory-driven. It is known to apply linguistic theories, approaches, descriptions and methods to proffer solutions to 'real world problems in which language is a central issue' (McCarthy, 2001:1). The linguistic analysis done in this book has utilized four main theories of grammar – Traditional Grammar, Structural Grammar, Transformational Generative Grammar and Systemic Functional Grammar. This is very commendable as it has shown that all the theories and approaches have their merits and are still very relevant. The writer has also shown that anyone who requires a good knowledge of the English language needs to be familiar with all the theories of grammar in order to have a holistic view of the grammar of English.

The book also uses a lot of examples to illustrate the discussion and there are relevant revision exercises to help readers/learners monitor their comprehension of the topics. These two features (eclectic approach and exemplification/illustrations), among others, have enriched the pedagogic relevance of the textbook as an invaluable resource for grammar teaching and learning.

The AL approach has enhanced the quality of the book thereby making it useful for both teachers and learners of the grammar of English at secondary and tertiary levels of education in ESL contexts – both as material for classroom interaction and as a reference source. The author has here demonstrated his experience in the teaching of the English language in secondary and tertiary institutions in Nigeria for many years.

Professor Sola T. Babatunde
Department of English
University of Ilorin
January, 2021

PREFACE

Grammar is the bedrock of language studies. Any language student who has a good knowledge of grammar will, therefore, excel in his or her studies. Unfortunately, many students (including some teachers of language) dread courses that are related to grammar. This is especially true of students of English as a Second Language (ESL). One of the reasons that can be adduced for this fear is that grammar is deemed 'dry' or abstract by many. It has lots of rules and exceptions which change over time. The only solution, therefore, is to master both the rules and their exceptions and to keep abreast of latest developments in the field in order to do well as a student of English. I have written this book, a product of my several years of English teaching and research experience in both secondary and tertiary institutions of learning, to help douse the fear of such people by simplifying difficult concepts and by giving copious examples.

The book is intended as an introductory course text on English grammar for undergraduate and college of education students of English in Nigeria and in other countries where English is a second language. For undergraduate students, the book will be good for courses on basic English grammar offered at the lower levels and also provide the foundation needed to succeed in syntax courses offered at the higher levels. In addition, it will give students of English in Nigerian colleges of education, who offer various courses on English grammar, the needed solid foundation. Polytechnic students who take courses on the basic grammar of English and secondary school students who need early exposure to the rudiments of English grammar will equally find the book very useful. Finally, teachers of English at all the levels of education mentioned above will find the book an invaluable reference material.

Among the unique qualities of this book is the use of an eclectic approach. Thus, when necessary, insights are drawn from different theories of grammar to buttress our points. One of the reasons for doing this is to expose students of English to the basic tenets or principles of the various approaches to grammar. Another reason is to give them a holistic view of English grammar based on the different perspectives of the leading authorities on grammar.

The book is divided into three parts. Part One is concerned with that aspect of grammar commonly known as 'morphology'. It starts with morphological description (the morpheme) and ends with lexical description (the word). Part Two, with theoretical explanations on phrases, clauses and sentences, deals with the structural part of grammar called 'syntax'. Part Three, with the caption 'English Grammar in Use', discusses how grammatical structures are used and the problems that are associated with their usage.

I assure you of a worthwhile reading experience and welcome suggestions on how to improve future editions of the book.

Gideon Olushola Dada
January, 2021

Chapter One

INTRODUCTION

1.1 The Concept of Grammar

Grammar can be viewed from, at least, six different perspectives. Five of these perspectives have been cited from Tomori (1977) and explained below. The sixth definition, given by Osisanwo (2002), comes last. Meanwhile, note that most of these definitions represent different approaches to the study of grammar. We shall discuss them in turn.

First, grammar is 'the body of prescriptive statements about usages that are considered acceptable and those that are considered unacceptable in a particular language' (Tomori, 1977, p. 1). This is the view of grammar as 'linguistic etiquette ... since it has to do with people's social attitudes and values' (Yule, 1996, p. 87). It is also the view of Traditional Grammar about the concept of grammar.

Secondly, grammar is 'the body of descriptive statements about the morphological and syntactic structures of a language' (Tomori, 1977, p. 1). This is the opinion of Leonard Bloomfield about grammar because, according to him, the study of grammar involves both 'morphology' and 'syntax' (Tomori, 1977, p. 21). This definition can be associated with Structural Grammar.

In the third place, still according to Tomori (1977, p. 1) grammar is defined as 'a book embodying the morphological and syntactic rules of a particular language'. This is an extension of Bloomfield's definition above and, by implication, an extension of the view of Structural Grammar as well. By inference, therefore, this book you are reading is a grammar of English.

Furthermore, grammar refers to 'the quality of the knowledge of a language possessed by a speaker, as inferred from the nature of his utterances' (Tomori, 1977, p. 1). This, according to Yule (1996, p. 87), is 'mental grammar' because the knowledge of a language possessed by a speaker is resident in his or her brain. This same view of grammar refers to 'linguistic competence' (Olujide, 1999, p. 49) because it is the *ability* that an individual has for language use. This is the view of Transformational Generative Grammar about grammar.

Moreover, grammar can be defined as 'a body of descriptive statements about the systemic interrelationships of structures within [a] language' (Tomori, 1977, p. 1). This view of grammar can be attributed to Systemic Functional Grammar.

Finally, according to Osisanwo (2002, p. 1), grammar also means 'the totality of language description'. This is the sixth definition of grammar. It is also the broadest of the definitions because it encompasses not only the theoretical levels of language description such as phonology, morphology, syntax and semantics but also the applied levels of language analysis such as pragmatics, stylistics, sociolinguistics and psycholinguistics. It is in this sense that 'grammar' is synonymous with 'linguistics'.

This book synthesizes basic insights from different theories of grammar and it is, therefore, related to all these definitions in varying degrees. Our next focus is on the different theories of grammar, which most of the definitions above are based on.

1.2 Theories of Grammar

The four main theories of or approaches to grammar, which are also relevant to this book, are summarized below.

1.2.1 Traditional Grammar (TG), also known as Classical Grammar (CG), was the approach to grammar inherited from Greek and Latin by early English grammarians such as Charles Butler, Roger Brawn, John Priestley, Lindley Murray, Robert Lowth, etc. (Osisanwo, 2002 & Egbe, 2005). Then, Greek and Latin were regarded as the most prestigious languages in the world and English grammar was only written to teach Latin to foreigners (Lamidi, 2016). Although Traditional Grammar has been criticized for certain weaknesses, its heritage to modern grammar, such as technical linguistic terminology, has been indispensable. Hence, terms such as sentence, clause, phrase, noun, verb, adjective, tense, concord, subject, predicate, etc which came from TG are still being used today. Such technical terms are also used in this book.

1.2.2 Structural Grammar emerged as a reaction to the inadequacies of Traditional Grammar, the foremost of which is 'prescriptivism' (Lamidi, 2016, p. 8). The thrust of Structural Grammar is to study the structural peculiarities or idiosyncrasies of each language. The major contributions to this school of thought in Europe came from Ferdinand de Saussure, a Swiss linguist and the generally acclaimed father of modern linguistics (Osisanwo, 2002, p. 5). The American linguist, Leonard Bloomfield, who viewed language from the perspective of psychological behaviourism, also made significant contributions to structuralism. Among other things, the structuralists replaced the traditional term 'parts of speech' with 'word classes' and used Subject Verb Complement Object Adjunct (SVCOA), instead of the traditional Subject Predicate (SP), to describe the structure of sentences. These structuralist terms are also used in this book, where necessary.

1.2.3 Transformational Generative Grammar (TGG) is also called Transformational Grammar (TG) or Generative Grammar (GG). It is one of the two modern approaches to grammar and a reaction to the weaknesses of Structural Grammar. The proponent of TGG is Avram Noam Chomsky, an American linguist. Chomsky has proved that man possesses a unique creative productive linguistic capacity which is resident in his brain (Lyons, 1981, pp. 230-231). He, therefore, believes that language is a mental phenomenon and the job of a linguist is to study the intuition of an ideal native speaker of a language in order to know and explain his innate ability (competence) for language use (performance). To do this, Chomsky came up with various grammatical rules such as phrase structure rules, transformational rules, government and binding rules, etc. Where necessary, references are made to this grammatical model in this book.

1.2.4 Systemic Functional Grammar (SFG), also known as Systemic Grammar (SG), or Functional Grammar (FG) is the second modern approach to the study of grammar and a reaction to TGG. Its exponent is Michael Alexander Kirkwood Halliday, a British linguist, who is of the opinion that grammatical interpretations are subject to the social context of language use. Hence, language is more about acceptability than grammaticality (Lamidi, 2016, p.17). Among other things, Halliday identified four grammatical categories for describing any human language. They are: unit, class, structure and system. Halliday views grammar as a network of systems of interrelated contrasts, which is why Osisanwo (2002, p. 10) described Systemic Grammar as a 'generative non-transformational grammar'. Aspects of this grammatical model are also used in this book.

1.3 Grammatical Continuum

Systemic Grammar, in presenting 'unit' as a grammatical category, has described five grammatical units with a diagram popularly known as 'grammatical rankscale'. This can be illustrated as follows.

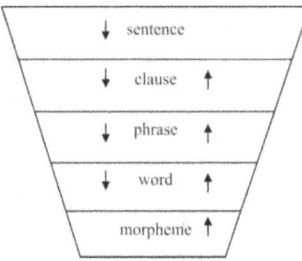

Figure 1: Grammatical Rankscale

The diagram above shows the units or components of grammatical description, in descending order, from 'sentence' and in ascending order, from 'morpheme'. According to the rankscale, the largest unit is 'sentence' while the smallest unit is 'morpheme'. A sentence is a combination of one or more clauses; a clause consists of one or more phrases; a phrase is made up of one or more words, and a word comprises one or more morphemes. However, Dada (2016, p. 1) has proposed a more realistic view of the grammatical rankscale with his 'sentence continuum', which we have re-named 'grammatical continuum', thus:

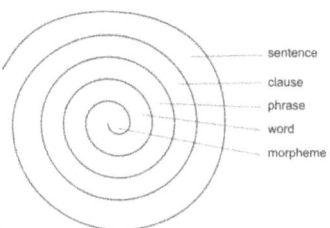

Figure 2: Grammatical Continuum

The diagram above presents the grammatical units in a cline. As in the rankscale, the morpheme is the smallest grammatical unit while the sentence is the largest unit. In addition, the spiral circle shows that each unit is capable of expanding or reducing. For example, the morpheme can expand into a word, the word can widen into a phrase, the phrase can spiral into a clause and the clause can grow into a sentence. Similarly, the sentence can reduce to a clause, the clause can reduce to a phrase, the phrase can decrease to a word and the word to a morpheme, all in a labyrinthine continuum and without any hindrance.

It should be noted, as the continuum implies, that the morpheme can further reduce to a smaller entity called 'phoneme' while the sentence can further expand to a larger unit called 'paragraph' (although, these two other units are not our focus in this book). This possibility of reduction or expansion explains why the spiral is not close-ended at both extremes. Also, we consider the use of a spiral circle (continuum) for the grammatical description here as better than the use of a rankscale or concentric circles (as used by some other grammarians) because each unit of a rankscale or each ring of concentric circles is compartmentalized, without the possibility of further growth or reduction.

1.4 Grammar and Syntax

Many students wrongly use the terms 'grammar' and 'syntax' interchangeably. However, from our second and third definitions of 'grammar' above, it should be clear that syntax is only an aspect of grammar, the other aspect being 'morphology'. While grammar has been defined above, morphology is dealt with in Chapter Two and we will, therefore, not repeat these definitions here. Rather, we will describe 'syntax' so as to distinguish it from 'grammar'. According to Tomori (1977, p. 21), 'syntax is the study of the rules governing the formation of linguistic units larger than the word.' The linguistic or grammatical units that are larger than the word are: the phrase, the clause and the sentence. Therefore, syntax is the study of phrases, clauses and sentences. In studying these units, we are interested in their elements, components or structure. Consequently, syntax is the study of the structure of phrases, clauses and sentences. This is the concern of Part Two of this book.

1.5 Eclecticism as Applicable to this Book

The notion of 'eclectic approach' (as we have in the title) adopted in this book refers to the use of principles from the four theories of grammar briefly described above. Therefore, this book does not exclusively use ideas from a single theory of grammar but rather, ideas which we consider best to explain our position on any given topic or concept are used, either from one or from a combination of the grammatical theories, when necessary. However, more emphasis is placed on Transformational Generative Grammar and Systemic Functional Grammar – the two internationally renowned modern approaches to grammatical analysis. For the sake of clarity, when a principle from a particular theory of grammar is used, the theory concerned is mentioned.

Revision Exercise 1

1. Define the term 'grammar' in any six ways that you have learnt about in this book. Which of the definitions do you consider as the widest in scope and why?
2. Illustrate the grammatical rankscale with any diagram of your choice and discuss the relationship among its units.
3. Briefly write on any three of these schools of grammar:
a. Traditional Grammar

b. Structural Grammar
c. Transformational Generative Grammar
d. Systemic Functional Grammar

PART ONE: MORPHOLOGY

Chapter Two

THE MORPHEME

2.1 The Morpheme and Morphology

a. go   b. ing
    book   s
    now   un
    happy   ly
    for   dis

Each of the items in (a) and (b) above is a morpheme. Fromkin, Rodman, Collins and Blair (1990), cited in Butt, Fahey, Spinks and Yallop (1995, p. 33), defined a morpheme as 'the minimal linguistic sign, a grammatical unit that is an arbitrary union of a sound and a meaning and that cannot be further analysed'. A morpheme may, therefore, be defined as the minimal meaningful grammatical unit of a language. It should be noted, according to the definition, that each of the morphemes listed in (a) and (b) above is not further divisible. We cannot, for instance, break the entity 'book' into *bo + ok or 'happy' into *ha + ppy or 'ing' into *i + ng because the divisions will not make any sense. (Note, henceforth, that an asterisk (*) is placed above an ungrammatical expression.) Also, the morphemes are meaningful e.g. 'ing' means or shows the progressive form of a verb (as in 'going'), 's' shows the plural form of a noun (as in 'apples') or the singular form of a verb (as in 'reads'), 'un' means 'not' in the word 'unhappy', 'ly' in 'badly' changes the adjective 'bad' to an adverb, 'dis' means 'not' in 'disallow', etc.

Morphology, on the other hand, 'is the subfield of linguistics that studies the internal structures of words and the relationships among words' (Akmajian, Demers, Farmer & Harnish, 2010, p.12). 'The internal structures of words', in the definition, implies 'morphemes'. Hence, morphology may also be defined as the study of morphemes. There is no clear distinction between a morpheme and a word but, for now, it will be helpful to know that morphemes are not words but some words are morphemes. This statement will be clearer as we progress in this chapter and in the next chapter where we have expatiated on the notion of 'word'.

2.2 Types of Morpheme

The diagram below illustrates the different types of morphemes in English. It is an improvement on that of Dada (2016, p. 4).

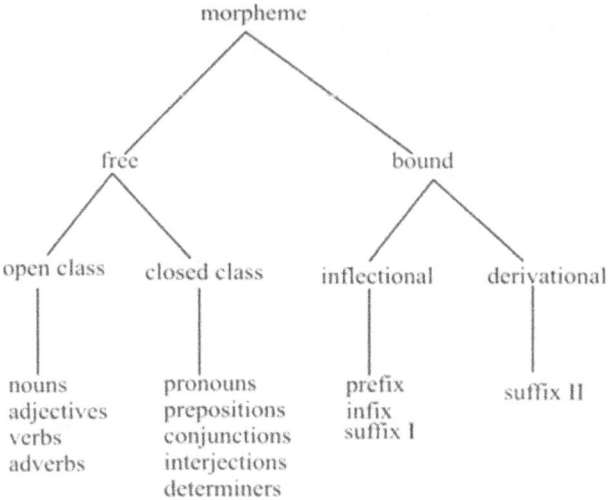

Figure 3: Morphological Tree

2.2.1 Free Morphemes

These are morphemes that can function independently as words. They do not have to be attached to other morphemes to function. They may, therefore, be proposed as *independent morphemes*. Free morphemes are broadly classified into open class words and closed class words. Items in the open class are nouns, adjectives, verbs and adverbs while those in the closed class are pronouns, prepositions, conjunctions, interjections and determiners. The free morphemes are, therefore, what we commonly know as 'parts of speech' from Traditional Grammar or 'word classes' from Structural Grammar. These free morphemes are elaborately discussed in the next chapter. Meanwhile, all the items listed in (a) under (2.1) above are free morphemes.

2.2.2 Bound Morphemes

These morphemes cannot stand alone as individual entities. They are usually added to words or free morphemes and they can thus be proposed as *dependent morphemes*. The items listed in (b) under (2.1) above are all bound morphemes. Bound morphemes, also known as affixes, are divided into inflectional morphemes and derivational morphemes.

a. **Inflectional Morphemes** are those that do not change the word class of words to which they are added. Inflectional morphemes may be prefixes, infixes or suffixes which are generally called affixes. 'Inflectional' is also spelt 'inflexional' in British English.

Prefixes, as the name suggests, are morphemes added to the beginning of words without altering the words' grammatical status i.e. without changing the grammatical class of the words.

Prefix	Base Word	New Word
un	fair (adj)	unfair (adj)

non	sense (noun)	nonsense (noun)
dis	regard (verb)	disregard (verb)
in	sane (adj)	insane (adj)
a	political (adj)	apolitical (adj)
de	freeze (verb)	defreeze (verb)
mis	understand (verb)	misunderstand (verb)
pseudo	democracy (noun)	pseudo-democracy (noun)
arch	angel (noun)	arch-angel (noun)
pre	marital (adj)	pre-marital (adj)

Infixes are morphemes that are inserted into words without changing their grammatical name or class. Some linguists opine that infixes do not exist or are rare in English (See Yule, 1996, p. 69; Odebunmi, 2006, p. 45 & Crystal, 2015, p. 243). However, Babatunde (2003, p. 117) and, Adedimeji and Alabi (2003, p. 37) regarded letters (morphemes) inserted in words, in place of other letters, so as to mark number or tense, as infixes. Such infixes are also known as 'replacive morphemes'. Examples of infixes are contained in the table below.

Infix	Base Word	New Word
e	man	men
e	fall	fell
ee	foot	feet
ee	goose	geese
a	come	came
a	sit	sat
a	sing	sang
o	write	wrote
o	drive	drove

| oo | stand | stood |

Suffixes: The suffixes concerned here are inflectional suffixes designated as suffix I, as opposed to derivational suffixes designated as suffix II, in the diagram on morphemes. Inflectional suffixes are added to the ends of words without effecting a change in word class. Below are examples of such:

Suffix	Base Word	New Word
er	London (noun)	Londoner (noun)
ship	relation (noun)	relationship (noun)
dom	king (noun)	kingdom (noun)
hood	brother (noun)	brotherhood (noun)
ful	hand (noun)	handful (noun)
ian	Christ (noun)	Christian (noun)
ry	slave (noun)	slavery (noun)
ist	style (noun)	stylist (noun)
ed	cook (verb)	cooked (verb)
ing	eat (verb)	eating (verb)

To conclude this sub-section, Akmajian, Demers, Farmer and Harnish (2010) pointed out that inflectional affixes are used to make word paradigms. A word paradigm refers to a set of the various forms of a word, as in the paradigm for the noun 'baby' (baby, baby's, babies, babies'), the paradigm for the verb 'take' (take, takes took, taken, taking) and the paradigm for the adjective 'cheap' (cheap, cheaper, cheapest). You might have noted that these paradigms describe ownership, number, tense and comparison. Thus, we can say that the main functions of inflectional affixes in English are to show ownership, number, tense and comparison.

    b. **Derivational Morphemes**, on the other hand, are those that change the word class of words to which they are added. Only suffixes (our suffix II) do this in English. A derivational suffix, therefore, is a morpheme that is added to the end of a word to change its grammatical category i.e. from one word class to another. The new word so formed is called 'derived word'. Study these examples of derivational suffixes.

Verb to Noun Suffixes

Suffix	Base Word (Verb)	Derived Word (Noun)
er	receive	receiver
or	act	actor
ant	defend	defendant
ee	employ	employee
tion	correct	correction
ment	move	movement
al	refuse	refusal

Noun to Adjective Suffixes

Suffix	Base Word (Noun)	Derived Word (Adjective)
ful	use	useful
less	mother	motherless
ly	friend	friendly
y	dirt	dirty
ish	child	childish
al	music	musical
ous	courage	courageous

Adjective to Noun Suffixes

Suffix	Base Word (Adjective)	Derived Word (Noun)
ness	good	goodness
ity	brief	brevity
ce	intelligent	intelligence
hood	false	falsehood
ster	young	youngster

Adjective to Verb Suffixes

Suffix	Base Word (Adjective)	Derived Word (Verb)
ify	simple	simplify
ize	popular	popularize
en	sweet	sweeten

Noun to Adverb Suffixes

Suffix	Base Word (Noun)	Derived Word (Adverb)
ward	south	southward
wise	clock	clockwise

2.3 Morphological Processes in English

One of the qualities of all languages is dynamism or creativity. This is because they are capable of accommodating new changes brought about by increase in human activities. This fact is even an understatement of the English language which has grown to be 'the most important language in the world today' (Banjo, 1996, p. 9)' with an estimated lexicon of about one million words and 'if all the science terminology were included, it could be twice that much' (Crystal, 1995, cited in Jackson, 2002, p. 4). The processes by which new words are created in a language are called 'morphological processes' or 'word-formation processes'. Below are morphological processes in English from Quirk and Greenbaum (1973), Yule (1996) and Jackson (2002).

1. **Affixation:** This is also called *derivation*. It is the process of forming new words by adding affixes (prefixes, infixes and suffixes) to base words. A word formed from this process is a 'derivative'. More than one affix may be involved in the creation of a derivative. Affixes have been discussed extensively in the previous section on bound morphemes and you are advised to refer to this section for details on them. However, for emphasis, a few examples of derivatives are given here while the affixes used in their creation are in bold.

   Prefixes: **dis**loyal, **un**tie, **im**proper, **il**legal, **mal**treat, **de**freeze, **over**confident, etc.

   Infixes: s**a**t, t**ee**th, wr**o**te, st**oo**d, s**a**ng, etc.

   Suffixes: harm**ful**, friend**ship**, free**dom**, jump**ing**, class**es**, convert**ed**, etc.

2. **Compounding:** This is the process of forming new words by combining two or more separate words (bases). A word so formed is called 'compound'. We propose three types of compounds: *block compounds, hyphenated compounds* and *open compounds*. Block compounds are written as a single orthographic word such as airtime, footprint, textbook, handwriting, etc. On the other hand, hyphenated compounds contain a hyphen e.g. foot-

dragging, self-control, bitter-sweet, story-telling, etc. Open compounds appear as separate words, such as washing machine, firing squad, cooking gas, walking stick, etc. When in doubt, consult a good dictionary of English to know when a compound should be block, hyphenated or open. Compounds may be nouns such as father-in-law, carry-over, firing squad, etc; they may be adjectives e.g. hard-working, lion-hearted, good-for-nothing, etc; they may be verbs such as baby-sit, sleep-walk, gainsay, etc and they may be adverbs e.g. non-stop, inside out, willy-nilly, etc.

3. **Conversion:** This refers to the process of forming a new word by changing the grammatical class of an existing word. The new word class thus becomes a new word. For instance, the following words, which are normally nouns, can also be used as verbs, depending on their context of use: bottle, can, butter, cement, increase, answer, beat, change, drink, fight, end, master, etc.

4. **Blending:** Here, parts of two separate words are combined to make another word. This is typically done by joining the beginning of one word to the end of another e.g. brunch (breakfast + lunch), edutainment (education + entertainment), motel (motor + hotel), telecast (television + broadcast), etc. A word resulting from this process is a 'blend'. Rarely though, blends can also result from the first part of two words as in forex (foreign + exchange).

5. **Clipping:** This occurs when a word of more than one syllable is shortened or reduced to create another word. To have a clipped word, the reduction may occur at the beginning of the word as in 'phone' (telephone), 'plane' (aeroplane); it may occur at the end of the word as in 'photo' (photograph), 'ad' (advertisement), 'bra' (for

brassiere), 'tele' (for television) and it may be at both ends of the word as in 'flu' (for influenza), 'fridge' (for refrigerator). Names of persons are usually shortened through clipping e.g. Shola (Olushola), Alex (Alexander), Beth (Elizabeth). Clipping is typical of the informal style.

6. **Acronymy:** This refers to the process of creating acronyms. An acronym is a word formed from the initial letters of a group of words. Acronyms are sometimes alphabetized such as NTA (Nigerian Television Authority), ESL (English as a Second Language) and, as such, they are called 'alphabetisms' (Quirk & Greenbaum, 1973, p. 449). They may also be called *alphabetic acronyms*. But more typically, acronyms are pronounced as single words e.g. UNESCO (United Nations Educational, Scientific and Cultural Organization), WAEC (West African Examinations Council) etc. These may be called *pronounceable acronyms*. Some linguists refer to alphabetic acronyms as 'abbreviations' and pronounceable acronyms as 'acronyms' (See Swan, 2005, p. 2). Short forms of words such as Mr, e.g., St, are also acronyms. Acronyms are normally separated with full stops (also called 'periods') in American English but they are not in modern British English.

7. **Coinage:** This is also known as *neologism*. It is the invention of totally new words or assigning of new meanings to existing words. An expression resulting from this is also called 'coinage' or 'neologism'. Coinages are usually occasioned by social changes, development or the inadequacy of existing lexemes to express new ideas (Odebunmi, 2006, p. 48). For example, words such as mouse, boot, windows, software, desktop, cybersecurity, download, etc were coined with the invention of

computer technology. Coinages in Nigerian English include bean cake, go slow, bush meat, area boy, yahoo boy, 419, etc.

8. **Reduplication:** This is a compounding process of creating words in which a word is repeated either with slight changes or with no changes at all. Words formed through this process are called 'reduplicatives'. Reduplicatives resulting from slight changes are 'partial reduplicatives' while those resulting from exact repetition of the same word are 'total reduplicatives' (Adedimeji & Alabi, 2003, pp. 41-42). Examples of partial reduplicatives are: walkie-talkie, criss-cross, see-saw, tick-tock, tip-top, wishy-washy, hanky-panky, helter-skelter, hocus-pocus, willy-nilly, etc while those of total reduplicatives are: goody-goody, tom-tom, chin-chin, etc.

9. **Backformation:** Here, a word of one type (usually a noun) is reduced to form another word of a different type (usually a verb). It could, therefore, be said that the two morphological processes of clipping and conversion are involved in backformation. Backformed words include televise (from television), opt (from option), enthuse (from enthusiasm), liaise (from liaison), revise (from revision), etc.

10. **Borrowing:** It is the act of taking a word from one language and adding it to the vocabulary of another language, with or without alteration to its spelling and pronunciation. Borrowing is a common feature of languages as no language is independent of influence from other languages. In relation to English, Medubi (2007, p. 10) observed that '… there is hardly any major language that has not contributed to the potpourri of Modern Standard English'. A word so borrowed is called

'loan word' e.g. alcohol (from Arabic), boss (from Dutch), robot (from Czech), tea (from Chinese), fiancé (from French), tycoon (from Japanese), mosquito (from Spanish), etc.

2.4 Segmentability of Morphemes

This refers to the separation of multi-morphemic entities into their component morphemes. According to Tomori (1977), segmentability of words (morphemes) is of three types thus:

   a. **Clear segmentability** occurs in words such as children (child + ren), asked (ask + ed), disengage (dis + engage), etc since it is easy to separate the morphemes in the words.

   b. **Unclear segmentability** is found in words such as wisdom (wise + dom), detention (detain + tion), behavour (behave + iour), etc because the words cannot be easily segmented into their component morphemes. In these examples, 'wis', 'deten' and 'behav' are referred to as 'bound alternants' (Tomori, 1977, p. 31) of the morphemes 'wise', 'detain' and 'behave' respectively.

   c. **Irregular segmentability** occurs with irregular words such as best (good + est, the superlative morpheme), saw (see + ed, the past tense morpheme), feet (foot + s, the plural morpheme).

2.5 Other Terminology in Morphology

   a. **Root:** It is the core or the heart of a word left when all affixes have been removed. This means the root is found in more than one morpheme. For instance, the root of the word 'internationally' is 'nation' while that of 'organization' is 'organ'.

b. **Base:** This refers to the basic form of a word before morphological rules (such as affixation, compounding, etc) are applies to it. A base (word), therefore, has a simple form with no additional free or bound morpheme. This means that a base word is a single morpheme. Examples of bases are call, go, shop, king, friend, etc.

c. **Stem:** It is the part of a word that inflectional affixes are attached to (Crystal, 2015, p. 452) or the part remaining after all inflectional affixes have been removed (Adedimeji & Alabi 2003, p. 44). The stem may have one or more morphemes. Thus, in 'unhappy', we have the stem 'happy' and in 'unhappiness' we have the stem 'happiness' because 'un' is inflectional. Note that the 'ness' in the word is derivational.

d. **Derived Word:** This is made up of at least one root and one or more free or bound morphemes. Tomori (1977, p. 34) gave the following morphological possibilities of derived words:

   i. One root and bound morpheme(s) e.g. the word 'interrelationship' has the root morpheme 'relate', the prefix 'inter' and the suffixes 'ion' and 'ship'; unemployment has the root 'employ', the prefix 'un' and the suffix 'ment'.

   ii. Two or more roots e.g. 'bookshop' (book, shop), 'merry-go-ground' (merry, go, round), 'roundabout' (round, about), etc.

   iii. Two or more roots and bound morpheme(s) e.g. 'bookshops' has two roots (book, shop) and one suffix (s), 'songwriters' has two roots (song, write) and two suffixes (er, s), singer-songwriters has three roots (sing, song, write) and three suffixes (er, er, s).

e. **Additive Morpheme:** An additive morpheme is an appendage or attachment to another morpheme e.g. in 'movement', 'calling' and 'lawful', the morphemes 'ment', 'ing' and 'ful' are additive morphemes.

f. **Replacive Morpheme:** Consider these sets of words: come - came, see - saw, man - men, and foot - feet. You would notice in the given words that some letters only replaced some other letters to form the past tenses of 'come' and 'see' and the plural forms of 'man' and 'foot'. Those letters are replacive morphemes. Replacive morphemes, therefore, are morphemes used in place of letters in words in order to change their grammatical category. Replacive morphemes are infixes.

g. **Empty Morpheme:** These are morphemes which are physically or orthographically present in words but have no meaning. In other words, 'they have a form but no function' (languagelinguistics.com/2014/06/19/empty-morphemes-in-linguistics/).Empty morphemes are usually inserted into words for phonological convenience i.e. to ease the pronunciation of words. Hence, they can be said to be phonologically significant but semantically inconsequential. Examples of empty morphemes in English include 'o' in thermometer, 'u' in factual, 'a' in systematic, etc.

h. **Suppletion:** This is a kind of replacive morpheme whereby there is a complete change in the form of the replaced word e.g. the word 'good' is changed to 'better' and 'best' to form its comparative and superlative degrees respectively. 'Better' and 'best' are, thus, suppletions.

i. **Morphs and Allomorphs:** Yule (1996, p. 79) proposed the term 'morphs' to refer to the actual forms used to realize morphemes and 'allomorphs' as the various forms of a morph based on different contexts or environments of use. Thus, we may talk of the plural morph as having the allomorphs 's', 'es', 'ies', 'en' and the zero-morph in 'shops', 'foxes', 'ladies', 'oxen' and 'sheep' respectively. Similarly, the past tense morph has the allomorphs 'd', 'ed' and the zero-morph in 'lived', 'called' and 'put' respectively. Irregular plural and past tense forms can be realized, for example, as tooth + plural (teeth) and see + past (saw).

j. **Pseudo-morpheme**: It is part of a word that appears like a morpheme but is not a morpheme in reality because it cannot be assigned an independent meaning or grammatical function. In other words, a pseudo-morpheme has no identifiable root word to which it is attached. Examples of pseudo-morphemes in English include:

    con as in conclude, conceive, condition, contain, conceal, etc.

    re as in repeat, receive, remit, reduce, reverse, etc.

    de as in destroy, delete, deter, defer, etc.

    ful as in grateful, etc.

    dis as in discuss, etc.

Note that the above pseudo-morphemes are genuine bound morphemes in: **con**figure, **re**new, **de**freeze, power**ful** and **dis**agree because the roots of the words are respectively 'figure', 'new', 'freeze', 'power' and 'agree'. However, in the examples of pseudo-morphemes given above, the same entities are not real morphemes. To prove that they are not bound morphemes, separate them from the words and you will discover that the remaining parts of the words are meaningless. For example, what is the meaning of 'dition' in 'condition', 'peat' in 'repeat', 'stroy' in 'destroy', 'grate' in 'grateful' or 'cuss' in 'discuss'? Therefore, entities such as 'dition', 'peat', 'stroy', etc which look like root morphemes in the examples above, are also pseudo-morphemes.

Revision Exercise 2

1. What is a morpheme?
    a. Prove, as convincingly as possible, the assertion that every word is a morpheme but not every morpheme is a word.
2. Distinguish between these types of morphemes and give five examples of each:
    a. Free Morpheme and Bound Morpheme
    b. Inflectional Morpheme and Derivational Morpheme
3. Write short notes on the following concepts in morphology with relevant examples:
    a. Additive morpheme
    b. Replacive morpheme
    c. Suppletion
    d. Pseudo-morpheme
    e. Empty morpheme
4. Differentiate convincingly between the terms below:
    a. Root and Stem
    b. Base Word and Derived Word
    c. Morph and Allomorph
5. Describe any six morphological processes of your choice and cite two examples of each.

6. Mention and explain the morphological processes involved in the creation of:
   a. COVID-19
   b. revise
   c. hanky-panky
   d. internalize
7. What is segmentability of morphemes?
   a. Explain three ways in which morphemes can be segmentalized.
   b. Segmentalize the following words:
      i. fishermen's
      ii. worst
      iii. kingfishers
      iv. retention
      v. bought

Chapter Three

THE WORD: THE OPEN CLASS

3.1 Word Classes in English

A word, according to Leonard Bloomfield, in Crystal (2015, p. 522), is 'a minimal free form'. In contrast to the word, therefore, a morpheme is a minimal free or bound form. While a word is always free, a morpheme may either be free or not. The word is next to the morpheme up the grammatical rankscale. Every word is made up of one or more morphemes. Other terms that are synonymous with 'word' in linguistics are *lexeme* and *lexical item*.

The term 'word classes' was coined by structural grammarians in place of the traditional term 'parts of speech'. Either of these terms refers to the roles that words play in the structure of sentences. Again, traditionally, there are eight classes of words: noun, adjective, verb, adverb, pronoun, preposition, conjunction and interjection. However, modern grammarians have added the ninth class of 'determiners'. Note that what we refer to as word classes here are captured as 'free morphemes' in the previous chapter and they are broadly grouped into two: 'open class' and 'closed class' or 'closed system' (Quirk & Greenbaum, 1973, p. 19). These two classes are also known as 'major' word classes and 'minor' word classes respectively (Leech & Svartvik, 2012, p. 417). The open class will be discussed in this chapter while the closed class will be discussed in the next chapter.

3.2 The Open Class

In the open class (of words), we have, nouns, adjectives, verbs and adverbs. The membership of the word classes in the open class is inexhaustible. In other words, the word classes are infinitely extendable because they are open to invention or creation of new lexical items as needs arise. Consequently, their membership cannot be numbered. For example, it is impossible to list all the nouns in English. Words in the open class are also called 'lexical' or 'content' words (Yule, 1996, p. 76). They are content words because they 'contain' or express more meaning than the words in the closed class. As Yule (1996, p. 76) put it, they 'carry' the 'content' of the messages we 'convey'.

There are two senses in which the expression 'open class' is applicable. One, the four parts of speech mentioned above can be seen as constituting a group of word classes with unlimited membership. Two, each word class can also be seen as an open class because its members are innumerable and, as such, there are four open classes (of words). We shall discuss them in turn.

3.2.1 Nouns

According to Halliday and Matthiessen (2014, p. 59), nouns refer to 'entities'. Entities have names and so, nouns can also be seen as names. These may be names of persons, animals, places, things, ideas, emotions, and so on e.g. Gideon, dog, Abuja, stone, hunger, interest, etc.

Features of Nouns

a. Most nouns are either countable or uncountable.
b. Most nouns can be differentiated based on sex or gender.

c. Most nouns have inflectional suffixes such as -s, -es, etc to show plurality.
d. Many nouns have derivational suffixes such as -tion, -ment, -ness, etc.
e. They are usually pre-modified by determiners like many, much, the, etc.

Types of Nouns

1. **Countable nouns:** These are nouns that can be numbered, also known as 'count nouns' e.g. children, eggs, mangoes, houses, trees, books, birds, stones, etc. Countable nouns can be in singular or plural form. When they are plural, they take such plural inflections as '-s', '-es', etc. This is discussed elaborately under 'Number category in Nouns'.

2. **Uncountable nouns:** They are nouns that cannot be numbered and are also known as 'non-count' or 'mass nouns'. Examples of uncountable nouns are: water, oil, sugar, love, interest, fatigue, hunger, etc. Unlike countable nouns, uncountable nouns are neither singular nor plural.

Note that the following nouns are regarded and used as uncountable nouns: equipment,

property (belongings), furniture, luggage, news, information, advice, behaviour, damage,

evidence, accommodation, slang, jargon, machinery, stationery. To count them, learn to use

expressions like *an item/a piece of* ... or *five items/pieces of* ... as in:

There are *four pieces of furniture* in the room – a chair, a table, a stool and a bed.

Note also that certain uncountable nouns are used as countable nouns in technical parlance e.g.

- moneys/monies (meaning 'sums of money')
- waters (for seas or oceans)
- fats and oils (as a class of food)
- sugars (such as glucose, lactose, sucrose, etc)
- properties (qualities of something)
- works (as in Ministry of Works or works of art)

3. **Concrete nouns** are tangible nouns because they appeal to the senses of touch and sight. In other words, such nouns can be seen and touched e.g. book, chair, goat, ruler, shoe, flower, man, kerosene, etc.

4. **Abstract nouns** are intangible i.e. they cannot be touched nor seen. They include truth, love, wisdom, joy, fear, interest, peace, chaos, courage, etc.

5. **Proper nouns** are specific names of persons, animals, places and things. They are nouns that have unique reference. Sub-classes of proper nouns include:

   i. names of persons e.g. Tayo, David, Shola, Isaac, etc.

   ii. names of places (towns, cities, countries, etc.) e.g. Jos, Lagos, Ghana, Africa, etc.

   iii. days of the week e.g. Monday, Wednesday, Friday, etc.

   iv. months of the year e.g. January, April, December, etc.

v. names of specific animals (pets) e.g. Jack (a dog), Bob (a monkey), etc.

vi. languages e.g. English, Yoruba, Chinese, Arabic, etc.

vii. festivals e.g. Osun Festival, Christmas, Easter, Ramadan, etc.

viii. names of bodies of water (rivers, lakes, seas, oceans, etc.) e.g. River Niger, Kainji Dam, Atlantic Ocean, Red Sea, etc.

ix. names of hills, mountains e.g. Zuma Rock, Mount Everest, Mount Olive, etc.

Note that the first letter of a proper noun should be capital.

6. **Common nouns**, on the other hand, are general names of persons, animals, places and things e.g. father, girl, lion, room, hall, captain, shoe, student, etc.

7. **Collective nouns** are names of groups of persons, things, etc. for instance, audience, army, panel, swarm, pride (of lions), bevy (of ladies), choir, fleet, herd, staff, jury, committee, etc. Note that either a singular or plural verb can be used with most singular collective nouns, depending on the context of use. (See the section on 'notional concord' for more on this.)

8. **Compound nouns** consist of two or more words used to refer to a single noun. Most compound nouns are hyphenated e.g. mother-in-law, passer-by, managing-director, step-mother, etc. Many people have a problem with the plural forms of compound nouns. This is discussed under the section on plurals of compound nouns.

9. **Gerunds** are nouns in the form of verbs and are sometimes called verbal nouns. They have final 'ing' like

verbs in their progressive forms but are used as nouns. Examples of these are those italicized in the following sentences:

I prefer *reading* to *writing*.

Running is an exercise.

Mr Dada likes *teaching*.

Functions of Nouns

Nouns generally function as subject, object, and complement in sentences. The following are the specific functions of nouns and the italicized item is the noun in question in each case:

a. **Noun as subject of a verb:** This is a noun as the doer of an action e.g. *The hawk* killed a snake ('The hawk' as the subject of the verb 'killed')

b. **Noun as direct object of a verb:** This noun is the primary receiver of the action of a verb e.g. Mary gave Dara *some money*. ('some money' as the direct object of the verb 'gave')

c. **Noun as indirect object of a verb:** It is the secondary receiver of the action of a verb e.g. Mary gave *Dara* some money ('Dara' as the indirect object of the verb 'gave'). For more explanation on direct and indirect objects, see the section on transitive verbs.

d. **Noun as complement of a subject:** This is a noun which adds to the meaning of another noun (subject) e.g. The lady is *a nurse*. ('a nurse' as complement of the subject 'the lady')

e. **Noun as complement of an object:** This is a noun that describes the sentence object e.g. The students made John the captain. ('the captain' as complement of the object 'John').

f. **Noun in apposition to a subject:** When two nouns are co-referential (used to refer to the same thing), the second is said to be in apposition to the first e.g.

  i. Dr Shaw, *the principal*, is American.

  In the above sentence, 'the principal' is in apposition to the subject 'Dr Shaw'. However, consider the following sentence:

  ii. Dr Shaw, the principal is American.

  While in (i) above, 'Dr Shaw' and 'the principal' refer to the same person, in (ii), someone is telling Dr Shaw about an American principal.

a. **Noun in apposition to an object:** This happens when another noun (phrase) is used in reference to the object of the sentence e.g.

  He beat Jack, *a stubborn boy*.

  Here, 'a stubborn boy' is appositional to the object, 'Jack'.

Case Category in Nouns

Case is a grammatical category which reflects the grammatical function of a word in a group of words. Thus, case in nouns shows the grammatical relationship between a noun and another word in a group of words. In modern English grammar, three types of case are recognized and they are:

1. **Nominative Case:** Also called subjective case, this occurs when a noun is used as the subject of a sentence e.g. *Eric* bought the house.

2. **Accusative Case:** This is when a noun is used as the object of a sentence. It is also called objective case e.g. Eric bought *the house*.
3. **Genitive Case:** This is when a noun is used to show ownership and it is also called possessive case e.g. There is *Olu's* car. OR There is the car *of Olu*. ('Olu's' and 'of Olu' are in genitive case). As exemplified, there are two kinds of genitive case: the '-s genitive' and the 'of-genitive'.

Number Category in Nouns

One of the characteristics of countable nouns is that number can be marked in them i.e. they can either be singular (one) or plural (more than one). There are both regular and irregular plural forms. Nouns with regular plural forms have a predictable pattern while irregular nouns do not.

Nouns with Regular Plural Forms

The countable nouns in this class take the suffix –s or –es.

a. Nouns that take the 's' inflection include:

Singular	Plural
car	cars
girl	girls
day	days
bird	birds
room	rooms

b. Those that take the '-es' inflection include words that end in the letters **s, h, o** or **x**:

bus   buses

church churches
mango mangoes
fox foxes
echo echoes

Note that these nouns are only pluralized with the addition of 's': ratio, solo, logo, photo, kilo, piano, avocado and commando.

Nouns with Irregular Plural Forms

c. These include nouns that end in a consonant sound plus letter 'y'. The letter 'y' is replaced with 'i' and 'es' is added to pluralize the word.

lorry lorries
baby babies
lady ladies
city cities

d. The final 'f' or 'fe' is replaced with 'ves' in these nouns:

wife wives
life lives
calf calves
half halves
thief thieves

e. Note that the following nouns have regular plural forms:

chief chiefs
safe safes
proof proofs
roof roofs

f. These have dual plural forms:

scarf	scarfs/scarves
dwarf	dwarfs/dwarves
hoof	hoofs/hooves
handkerchief	handkerchiefs/handkerchieves
fish	fish/fishes

'Fishes' here refers to different species of fish.

g. Some nouns have their inner vowels changed in various ways for plurality:

man	men
goose	geese
tooth	teeth
foot	feet
mouse	mice
louse	lice

h. For some nouns, 'en' is added to form their plurals:

child	children
ox	oxen

Zero Plurals

These are nouns that have the same form both in the singular and in the plural e.g. sheep, deer, aircraft, series, species, dozen, dice, data, etc.

Note: The singular of 'dice' in American English is 'die' but its plural remains 'dice' as in British English.

Pluralia Tantum

'Pluralia tantum' is an Italian expression which means 'plural only' and its singular form is 'plurale tantum' (http://en.m.wikipedia.org/wiki/plurale-tantum). Pluralia tantum, therefore, refers to nouns without singular forms or nouns that only appear or are only used in the plural. Examples of these include: alms, arms (weapons), species, annals, archives, arrears, barracks, crossroads, funds, goods, manners, means, minutes (of a meeting), premises, riches, savings, thanks, surroundings, headquarters, outskirts, binoculars, pliers, scissors, trousers, shorts, spectacles, pants, pyjamas, odds, quarters, congratulations, etc.

Pluralia tantum can be divided into two: those that take singular verbs and those that take plural verbs. With the above list of pluralia tantum, plural verbs are normally used e.g.

Arms were used by children during the civil war.

The available *funds are* not enough for the project.

The *goods have* been delivered.

Riches make proud.

On the other hand, with the following sets of pluralia tantum, singular verbs are usually required:

- **Diseases**: rickets, rabies, mumps, diabetes, measles, shingles, AIDS, etc.
- **Subjects/Activities**: mathematics, linguistics, economics, politics, logistics, statistics, etc.
- **Games/Sports**: draughts, snakes and ladders, billiards, darts, fives, aerobics, athletics, gymnastics, dominoes, etc.

- **Place names**: Athens, Algiers, Wales, Brussels, United States, etc.
- **Others**: news, summons, gallows, series, means, species, windows (in computing), etc.

Examples in sentences:

Measles kills many children annually.

Mathematics is difficult.

The *news was* broadcast by Cyril Stober.

Note that the term *singularia tantum,* meaning words that only have singular forms, is only applicable to mass or non-count nouns such as peace, anger, tea, honesty, love, joy, etc and its singular form is *singulare tantum.*

Plurals of Compound Nouns

To pluralize compound nouns, 's' is added to the most important word(s) in the group and this/these may be at various positions in the group, thus:

a. **Plural in first position**

commander-in-chief	commanders-in-chief
daughter-in-law	daughters-in-law
father-in-law	fathers-in-law
runner-up	runners-up
passer-by	passers-by
man-of-war	men-of-war
head of state	heads of state

b. **Plural in first or last position**

attorney general	attorneys general/ attorney generals
mouthful	mouthsful/mouthfuls
spoonful	spoonsful/spoonfuls

c. Plural in both first and last positions

manservant	menservants
woman doctor	women doctors
gentleman teacher	gentlemen teachers

d. Plural in last position

deputy governor	deputy governors
vice president	vice presidents
girlfriend	girlfriends
woman hater	woman haters
grown-up	grown-ups
man-eater	man-eaters

Note that if you have the structure: article + number + hyphen + noun in a compound pre-modifier, the noun after the hyphen should be singular e.g. a ten-man committee, an eight-person panel, the five thousand-soldier battalion, etc.

Foreign Plurals

These are nouns that are borrowed from other languages into the English language, most of which have retained their original foreign spellings.

Nouns of Greek Origin

metropolis	metropolises
basis	bases

analysis	analyses
crises	crises
diagnosis	diagnoses
hypothesis	hypotheses
oasis	oases
demon	demons
criterion	criteria
phenomenon	phenomena

Nouns of Latin Origin

Singular	Plural
alumnus (male)	alumni (male)
alumna (female)	alumnae (female)
radius	radiuses/radii
syllabus	syllabuses/syllabi
formula	formulas/formulae
antenna	antennas/antennae
larva	larvae
album	albums
stadium	stadiums/stadia
ultimatum	ultimatums/ultimate
curriculum	curriculums/curricula
stratum	strata
memorandum	memorandums/memoranda
symposium	symposiums/symposia
medium	media
index	indexes/indices
apex	apexes/apices
appendix	appendixes/appendices
matrix	matrixes/matrices

genius   geniuses

Note: For nouns that have both regular and foreign plural variants, the regular plurals are used in general or everyday English while the foreign plurals are used in technical contexts e.g. 'feed formulas' (for preparing animal feeds) but 'mathematical formulae' (in mathematics).

Nouns in Generic Reference

Nouns can be used to include all members of a particular group. These are nouns in generic reference and there are two main ways this happens:

    a. By combining 'the' with a nationality noun e.g. the British = British people; the Portuguese = Portuguese people; the Chinese = Chinese people

    b. By combining 'the' with an adjective e.g. the poor = poor people; the good and the bad= good people and bad people; the blind = blind people; the deaf = deaf people

Note: The plural of Mr (Mister) is Messrs as in: Messrs Iyiola, Obi and Alfa are absent.

Gender Category in Nouns

One of the distinctive features of many nouns, especially humans and animals, is that they can be distinguished based on sex. The male gender is typically called 'masculine', the female gender is called 'feminine' while 'neuter' refers to inanimate objects which are neither male nor female.

Masculine	Feminine
king	queen
actor	actress

hero	heroine
wizard	witch
nephew	niece
dog	bitch
cock	hen
gander	goose
lion	lioness
bull	cow

Special Cases of Gender

- Note that when we refer to countries as political or economic units, the feminine pronoun 'she' or 'her' is used e.g. Nigeria got *her* independence in 1960.

- Likewise, when ships or even cars are mentioned with affection or pride, they are feminine e.g. The ship is new; when is *she* sailing?

- On the contrary, a female owner of such a ship or car may use 'he' for it, regarding it as masculine (Quirk & Greenbaum, 1973) thus:

    John: Where is your car?

    Mary: He is in the garage.

Revision Exercise 3

1. State any three features of nouns that you have learnt about.
2. Explain any five kinds of nouns that you have read about.
3. What is the function of the italicized words in these sentences?

a. Seun plays the *guitar* skilfully.
b. Tell the stubborn girl, *Doris*, to come.
c. *Donald* won one gold and two silvers in the tournament.
d. The test of love is *sacrifice*.
e. The horse drank all the *water* in the bucket.

4. What is 'case' in grammar? Expatiate on these types of case in relation to English nouns:
   a. Nominative case
   b. Accusative case
   c. Genitive case
   d. Write the plural forms of these nouns: key, calf, safe, dwarf, goose, louse, deer, dozen, secretary-general, son-in-law, mouthful, manservant, grown-up, alumna, curriculum, medium, analysis, phenomenon, criterion, dice.

3.2.2 Adjectives

Consider these sentences:
1. My father has a *red* car.
2. Ayo bought a *long* ruler.
3. You are *lucky* today.
4. She is *beautiful*.

The words in italics in the above sentences describe certain nouns and pronouns. The word 'red' describes 'car' (a noun), 'long' describes 'ruler' (a noun), 'lucky' describes 'you' (a pronoun) and 'beautiful' describes 'she' (a pronoun). Words that describe nouns and pronouns as these are called adjectives. Adjectives, therefore, can be defined as words that describe or limit the use of nouns and pronouns. In other words, they are words that qualify or modify nouns and pronouns. Perhaps, this is why Halliday and Matthiessen (2014, p. 59) defined them as 'qualities'.

Features of Adjectives

1. All adjectives give information about nouns or pronouns.
2. Most adjectives are gradable i.e. they are used for comparison and so, have comparative and superlative forms e.g. big, bigger, biggest; good, better, best, etc.
3. Most adjectives have noun forms or equivalents e.g. good – goodness, beautiful – beauty, short – shortness, excellent – excellence, brave – bravery, etc.
4. The grammatical functions of most adjectives are contextual. i.e. they are only known as adjectives when used in sentences. This is because it is possible for other parts of speech such as noun, verb, adverb, etc. to function as adjectives e.g. my *engineer* son (noun as adjective), *stolen* car (verb as adjective), the *then* governor (adverb as adjective), etc.
5. Many adjectives have derivational suffixes such as 'able' in 'readable', 'al' in 'practical', 'ful' in 'truthful', etc.
6. They may also have inflectional prefixes such as 'il' (illegal), 'un' (unhappy) or inflectional suffixes such as 'er' (shorter), 'est' (biggest), etc.
7. Most adjectives can be used both attributively and predicatively thus:

a. Bill Gates is a *wealthy* man. (Attributive use: 'wealthy' qualifying the noun 'man')

b. The man is *wealthy*. (Predicative use: 'wealthy' qualifying the noun 'man')

Types of Adjectives

1. **Adjectives of Quality**: These are also known as descriptive adjectives, attributive adjectives or epithets. As the name implies, they are adjectives which describe the qualities or attributes of nouns or pronouns. Such qualities may be height, age, size, shape, colour, etc. They may also result from the user's perception or judgment of such nouns or pronouns. Examples of attributive adjectives are: tall, fat, small, good, handsome, intelligent, etc as we have in :

    a. Sharon is a *beautiful* girl.

    b. The trees are *tall*.

    c. *Good* children respect elders.

    d. The president lives in a *green* house.

2. **Compound Adjectives**: They are adjectives that consist of two or more words, usually hyphenated to describe a noun or pronoun. What is special about this class of adjectives is that words of any class can be combined to qualify a noun or pronoun. Examples of compound adjectives are: good-for-nothing, do-or-die, hungry-looking, dare-devil, up-to-date, fast-moving, better-late-than-never, six-year-old, English-speaking, well-to-do, etc as italicized in the following sentences:

    Don't mind the *good-for-nothing* fellow.

    My ambition is not a *do-or-die* affair.

Two *hungry-looking* dogs are at the gate.

3. **Absolute Adjectives**: These are adjectives that cannot be compared or graded. In other words, they do not have comparative (*deader, *more excellent) and superlative (*deadest, *most excellent) forms. Besides, they do not take intensifiers such as very, so, too, extremely, etc (*very dead, *too excellent). The logic behind absolutes is that they are considered as inherently comparative (e.g. inferior, superior) or inherently superlative (e.g. dead, excellent) and so, it will be redundant to add *er/more* to them as comparatives or *est/most* to them as superlatives. Absolute adjectives may also be called *total adjectives*. Examples of absolute adjectives are: excellent, correct, entire, equal, final, inferior, superior, perfect, ultimate, dead, alive, complete, digital, false, pregnant, wonderful, unique, etc. Apart from the above list, kathysteinermann,com/Musings/absolute/ suggested that most absolute adjectives either have prefixes or suffixes, or they are colours. In addition to the above clues to absolutes, we wish to note that all compound adjectives are also absolutes (*more happy-go-lucky, *very good-for nothing, etc.).

Apart from the above types of adjectives, we would like to propose *participial adjectives* and *nominal adjectives*.

4. **Participial Adjectives**: These are verbs, usually in their progressive and past forms, used as adjectives and they may, rightly, be called *verbal adjectives*. They are of two types.

    a. **Present participial adjectives** are verbs in their progressive forms functioning as adjectives, as in the following sentences:

The *protesting* workers were rounded up.

Wake up the *sleeping* boy.

A *rolling* stone gathers no moss.

b. **Past participial adjectives** are verbs in their past participle forms which function as adjectives, as these examples show:

Participial adjectives are *derived* adjectives.

Abandoned buildings litter the city landscape.

Jim bought a *stolen* car.

5. **Nominal Adjectives**: These are adjectives that are derived from nouns or nouns that function as adjectives. They are also divided into two:

   a. **Proper Adjectives**: These are adjectives that are formed from proper nouns e.g. French, English, Nigerian, Chinese, Yoruba, Ngas, etc as in:

   He is an *English* actor.

   Ngas people are hospitable.

   Mr Dennis is a *French* man.

   b. **Common Adjectives**: They are common nouns used as adjectives, as in these sentences.

   His *doctor* mother bought him a car.

   Malaria is a *killer* disease.

   Femi was my *childhood* friend.

   Janet's *politician* uncle has won the election.

Both participial adjectives and nominal adjectives can be called *derived adjectives* since they are derived from verbs and nouns respectively.

Positions of Adjectives

Attributive position: When an adjective comes before the noun or pronoun it modifies, it is said to be in attributive position and is, thus, an attributive adjective as in 7a above.

Predicative position: An adjective that comes after the noun or pronoun it modifies is in predicative position and is referred to as a predicative adjective as in 7b above.

Functions of Adjectives

The role of adjectives is to qualify or modify nouns and pronouns.

a. Adjectives qualifying nouns

   Write with a *black* pen.

   She has a *wild* dog.

In the sentences above, the adjective 'black' qualifies the noun 'pen' while 'wild' qualifies the noun 'dog'.

b. Adjectives qualifying pronouns

   I am *tired*.

   They are *hungry*.

   The pronouns 'I' and 'they' in the sentences above are qualified by the adjectives 'tired' and 'hungry' respectively.

Comparison of Adjectives

One of the characteristics of adjectives, as earlier stated, is that they can be used to show comparison between nouns. This happens in three ways called degrees of comparison of adjectives. First, a simple adjective used to describe a noun in isolation from any other noun is called 'positive'; second, an inflected adjective (with 'er' or 'more') used to compare between two nouns is called 'comparative' and third, the form of an adjective (with 'est' or 'most') used to compare three or more nouns is known as 'superlative'. Below is a list of such **regular adjectives**. Note that most of the adjectives that form their comparatives and superlatives with the addition of 'er' and 'est' are monosyllabic i.e. have one syllable.

Positive	Comparative	Superlative
tall	taller	tallest
big	bigger	biggest
fat	fatter	fattest
bold	bolder	boldest
wise	wiser	wisest
young	younger	youngest
great	greater	greatest
happy	happier	happiest
healthy	healthier	healthiest

Polysyllabic adjectives take 'more' and 'most' for comparison.

comfortable	more comfortable	most comfortable
powerful	more powerful	most powerful
beautiful	more beautiful	most beautiful
courageous	more courageous	most courageous
intelligent	more intelligent	most intelligent

The following adjectives have dual comparatives and superlatives:

handsome	handsomer	handsomest
	more handsome	most handsome
stupid	stupider	stupidest
	more stupid	most stupid
common	commoner	commonest
	more common	most common
wicked	wickeder	wickedest
	more wicked	most wicked
clever	cleverer	cleverest
	more clever	most clever

Other adjectives with dual comparatives and superlatives include: simple, cruel, polite, gentle, narrow, pleasant, etc.

Irregular adjectives do not follow the above pattern. They have comparative and superlative forms which have no fixed rules but must be learnt individually.

These include:

good, well	better	best
bad, evil	worse	worst
many	more	most
much	more	most
little	less	least
far	farther/further	farthest/furthest
in	inner	inmost/innermost
out	outer	utmost/uttermost
up	upper	upmost/uppermost
old	older/elder	oldest/eldest

Examples in sentences
1. George is *wise*.
2. Richard is *more courageous* than George.
3. Henry is the *handsomest/most handsome* of the three boys.

Note that it is wrong to combine 'more' with 'er' to form the comparative degree of an adjective and it is wrong to combine 'most' with 'est' for the superlative degree of an adjective. Thus, the following expressions are wrong.

*more bigger, *more wiser, *more better (double comparatives)

*most biggest, *most wisest, *most best (double superlatives)

Note on 'old' and its degrees of comparison: Although 'older' and 'oldest' are used for persons, animals and things, 'elder' and 'eldest' are only used for persons. Besides, the use of 'elder' and 'eldest' is strictly limited to family members. Finally, 'elder' is not followed by 'than' when used for comparison.

My dog is *older* (not elder) than yours.

Mine is the *oldest* (not eldest) town in the state.

Victor is the *oldest* or *eldest* of the couple's children.

Note, as discussed under types of adjectives, that absolute adjectives do not have comparatives and superlatives.

Order of Adjectives

Sometimes, two or more adjectives are used to describe a noun or pronoun. When this happens, the adjectives should be arranged in a conventionally correct pattern as given below. Note, however, that the order or arrangement is not completely fixed as

Swan (2005, p. 15) rightly observed. These are adjectives denoting:

1st General adjectives of subjective judgement e.g. good, brilliant, fast, etc.

2nd Size e.g. fat, big, small, slim, etc.

3rd Age e.g. young, old, new, etc.

4th Shape e.g. round, square, rectangular, oval, etc.

5th Colour e.g. blue, white, red, black, fair, etc.

6th Origin e.g. Nigerian, British, Yoruba, Igbo, etc.

7th Material e.g. silk, cotton, leather, wooden, clay, etc.

8th Nominal adjectives e.g. *lawyer* friend, *banker* sister, etc.

Then comes the noun/pronoun being described. Example:

    a. I have a smart big old black Alsatian dog.

    b. She is a beautiful slim young fair Yoruba musician.

Revision Exercise 4

1. List any four qualities of adjectives.
2. Discuss any three types of adjectives that you have read about.
3. Identify the comparatives and superlatives of these adjectives: wealthy, faithful, interesting, handsome, comfortable, good, much, little, up, far.
4. In each of the phrases below, arrange the given adjectives correctly to qualify the noun in brackets.

   black Nigerian young fat (girl)

   round clay new beautiful (pot)

tall fierce hungry Alsatian brown (dog)

3.2.3 Verbs

Examine these examples:
- a. Jackson *wrote* a letter.
- b. The lady *has* a bag.
- c. I *will come* tomorrow.
- d. It *is* cold.

The words in italics in the examples above are all verbs. The example in (a) is an action, that of (b) shows possession, that of (c) indicates mood while the one in (d) is a state of being. Verbs, therefore, usually have different meanings which is why some scholars tend to define them as action words, states of being, etc. However, we can also observe that all verbs, irrespective of their meaning or type, have one tense or another. Therefore, a verb can be defined as a word that shows tense.

Features of Verbs

a. Verbs have tenses or tense forms.

b. Verbs are obligatory elements of sentences.

c. Most of them, especially the main verbs, have independent meaning and can be used as minor sentences e.g. Go. Take. Sing. Come. Write. Jump. Shout.

d. Most verbs can have inflectional suffixes for different purposes e.g. 'ed', 'en', 'ing' (for tenses); 's', 'es' (for number).

e. They can take derivational suffixes such as: ate, ise/ize, fy, etc and derivational prefixes such as en-, out-, sure-, de-, etc.

Classification of Verbs

Various criteria have been used to classify English verbs and these include: regular and irregular verbs, transitive, intransitive and ergative verbs, lexical and auxiliary verbs, finite and non-finite verbs, dynamic and stative verbs, linking verbs and, phrasal verbs. We shall look at these one after the other.

1. **Regular and Irregular Verbs:** Regular verbs are those that form their past tenses and past participles by 'ed' inflection. This is why it is often said that all the forms of a regular verb can be stated once its base is known. For example:

Present Tense	Past Tense	Past Participle
jump	jumped	jumped
look	looked	looked
try	tried	tried
stop	stopped	stopped
mix	mixed	mixed

On the other hand, verbs whose past tenses and past participles are formed by a change of a vowel letter or letters, or in any other way, are irregular verbs. They include:

see	saw	seen
so	went	Gone
write	wrote	written
sing	sang	sung
cut	cut	cut

Types of Irregular Verbs

According to Wren and Martin (2010, p. 85), there are three types of irregular verbs, thus:

a. Verbs in which the present tense, the past tense and the past participle are all the same e.g. put, hit, bet, burst, hurt, read, split, cast, spread, shut, cut, let, sweat, broadcast, set, etc.

b. Verbs in which two of the three tenses are the same e.g. sit, say, bring, catch, build, beat, come, hang, have, light, pay, lose, get, tell, run, win, learn, teach, have, etc.

c. Verbs in which all the three tenses are different e.g. is, sing, ring, begin, bite, see, do, eat, drive, fall, give, go, hide, lie, speak, steal, take, write, throw, know, fly, ride, etc.

In addition to the three above, we shall propose the fourth type thus:

d. Verbs which have dual past tense and/or past participle forms e.g. burn, dream, dwell, get, hang, leap, learn, show, smell, spell, swell, wed, wet, as in the table below.

Present Tense	Past Tense	Past Participle
burn	burnt/burned	burnt/burned
dream	dreamt/dreamed	dreamt/dreamed
dwell	dwelt/dwelled	dwelt/dwelled
get	got	got/gotten
leap	leapt/leaped	leapt/leaped
learn	learnt/learned	learnt/learned
kneel	knelt/kneeled	knelt/kneeled
show	showed	shown/showed
smell	smelt/smelled	smelt/smelled
spell	spelt/spelled	spelt/spelled
spoil	spoilt/spoiled	spoilt/spoiled
swell	swelled	swollen/swelled
wed	wedded/wed	wedded/wed

wet	wet/wetted	wet/wetted

The second usages/spellings above, where there are two, are characteristic of American English.

2. **Transitive, Intransitive and Ergative Verbs**

   A. **Transitive Verbs** are verbs whose actions are received by an object. In other words, they are verbs that have an object (receiver of action). Fakuade (2012, p. 56) categorized them into verbs that denote: (Note that in the example sentences, the verbs are underlined while their objects are italicized)

   - Senses e.g. feel, see, hear, touch, taste, smell, perceive, etc as in 'I can see *a car* up the hill'.
   - Feelings e.g. admire, love, like, enjoy, fear, want, prefer, hate, frighten, scare, detest, etc as in 'Raymond fears *his father* a lot'.
   - Facts e.g. accept, investigate, believe, correct, forget, discuss, report, know, remember, interrogate, find, etc as in 'The accountant corrected *the figures*'.
   - People e.g. blame, beat, kill, thank, warn, please, try, convince, comfort, etc as in 'Warn *her* not to interfere in the affairs of others'.

Some transitive verbs may be used without an object. They include: accept, answer, change, choose, clean, cook, drive, eat, forget, help, iron, learn, pain, phone, read, sing, steal, study, type, understand, wash, watch, write, etc as in: 'Your wife *phoned* at 4pm.' 'Can you *read*?'

It should also be noted that only transitive verbs can be used with passive structures. This is discussed under active voice and passive voice. However, although 'have' is a transitive verb, it can only be used in the active e.g. 'She has a house' but not *'A house is had by her'.

Types of Transitive Verbs

Transitive verbs are divided into three: monotransitive verbs, ditransitive verbs and complex transitive verbs (Greenbaum, 1973, p. 14).

    a. **Monotransitive Verbs** are used with a single object (O) e.g.

    She <u>ate</u> (V) *the food* (O)

    Tim <u>wrote</u> (V) *that book* (O).

    b. **Ditransitive Verbs** are those that have two objects. While one is called 'direct object' (Od), the other is called 'indirect object' (Oi). A direct object is the first receiver of the action of the verb while an indirect object is the second receiver of the action of the verb.

    She has <u>written</u> (V) *Ben* (Oi) *a love letter* (Od).

    Daddy <u>sends</u> (V) *you* (Oi) *his love* (Od).

    They <u>showed</u> (V) *their house* (Od) to *us* (Oi).

    I <u>gave</u> (V) *the money* (Od) to *Tolu* (Oi).

    Our teacher <u>gave</u> (V) *us* (Oi) *an assignment* (Od).

    c. **Complex Transitive Verbs** have object complements (Co) as in the following examples:

    The voters elected (V) him (O) governor (Co).

    Year in year out, the students make (V) Andrew (O) the captain (Co).

Note that either a direct or an indirect object can come first in a sentence. A logical way to know the direct object is to ask yourself which of the objects is first affected by the action of the verb or receives the action of the verb first. For example, in the sentence 'I gave *the money* (Od) to *Tolu* (Oi),' the covert first receiver of the action of *giving* is 'the money' because it would first have to be *taken* before it could be *given* to 'Tolu'. Embedded or hidden in the meaning of the verb 'gave', therefore, is the verb 'took'. It is just like saying 'I took the money (first) and gave it to Tolu (second)'. Another way of distinguishing between these two types of object is that a direct object usually refers to something while an indirect object refers to somebody. (See the examples above.) Finally, the indirect object is sometimes preceded by a preposition such as 'to', 'for', etc.

Note, also, that the position of either object (direct or indirect) is not fixed. It all depends on how it is structured. For example, 'I gave the money (Od) to Tolu (Oi)' can be restructured as 'I gave Tolu (Oi) the money (Od)'. Note that the change in the positions of the objects in the two sentences has not changed their grammatical functions.

- **B. Intransitive Verbs** are those that do not normally take an object. Again, according to Fakuade (2012, p. 58), such verbs usually refer to:
  - Existence e.g. appear, die, live, occur, exist, happen, etc as in The patient *died* last night.
  - The human body e.g. ache, bleed, faint, smile, etc as in Musa's hand *bled* profusely from the accident.
  - Human noises e.g. cough, cry, laugh, scream, sight, snore, yawn, etc as in The panel of judges *laughed* uncontrollably.

- Light/Illumination e.g. glow, gleam, shine, spark, etc as in The car light *shines* brightly.
- Position/Movement e.g. move, come, depart, fall, leave, go, jump, run, sit, sleep, stand, swim, work, walk, etc as in The winner *swam* across the big river in five minutes.

It should be noted that intransitive verbs cannot be used in the passive but can only have *cognate objects* (Fakuade, 2012, p. 58) i.e. objects already suggested by the action of the verb. In the examples below, the verbs are underlined while their cognate objects are italicized.

The boy died a painful *death*.

The billionaire lived a meaningless *life*.

Aisha dreamt a bad *dream*.

C. **Ergative verbs** are verbs that can be used both transitively and intransitively. When such verbs are used transitively, they focus on the performer of the action but where they are used intransitively, the focus is on the receiver of the action. Such verbs include break, open, close, ring, start, stop, etc.

Transitive	Intransitive
The traffic warden *stopped* the car.	The car *stopped*.
His bodyguard *opened* the door.	The door *opened*.
I *broke* my cup.	My cup *broke*.

Note that the objects of the transitive verbs in the examples above are the subjects of the intransitive verbs.

3. **Lexical and Auxiliary Verbs:** Lexical verbs express actions and they can stand alone as meaningful entities when used as minor sentences. They are also referred to as 'main verbs' e.g. eat, write, see, go, sit, laugh, bath, teach, etc. On the other hand, **auxiliary verbs** do not express actions, neither can they be used as minor sentences. Instead, auxiliary verbs usually introduce or 'help' lexical verbs to express tense, number, mood, aspect, negation or question. This is why auxiliary verbs are also known as 'helping verbs'.

Types of Auxiliary Verbs

Auxiliary verbs are sub-classified into two: primary auxiliary and modal auxiliary verbs. We shall look at these in turn.

Primary Auxiliary Verbs: These are of three types: 'be', 'do' and 'have' verbs. The 'be' verb is of seven kinds (be, is, are, was, were, been, being), 'do' is of five kinds (do, does, did, done, doing) while 'have' is of four kinds (has, have, had, having). The various forms of the three primary auxiliary verbs showing number and tense are presented in the tables below:

Number

Verb	Singular	Plural
be	am	are
	is	are
	was	were
do	does	do
have	has	have

Tense

Verb	Present	Past	Perfect	Progressive
be	is	was	been	being
	are	were	been	being
do	does	did	done	doing
	do	did	done	doing
have	has	had	had	having
	have	had	had	having

Modal Auxiliary Verbs: These are also known as 'modal auxiliaries', 'modal verbs' or simply, 'modals'. Apart from indicating tense, another function of modal verbs is showing modality such as necessity, possibility, certainty, obligation, probability, request, permission, willingness, ability and so on (Murthy, 2012, pp. 127 & 133). So, unlike primary auxiliary verbs which mark tense and number, modal auxiliary verbs mark tense and modality, otherwise called functions or uses of modal verbs in the tables below. Another difference between primary and modal auxiliary verbs is that the former take inflections but the latter do not.

English modal auxiliaries are: can, could, may, might, shall, should, will, would, must, ought to, used to, need, dare, (Leech & Svartvik, 2012, p. 256), had better, tend to (Quirk and Greenbaum, 1973, p. 26), have to (Hornby, 2015) and 'had to' may be added to the list. From the list, you would note that 'can', 'may', 'shall', 'will' and 'have to' have their corresponding past forms as 'could', 'might', 'should', 'would' and 'had to'. The table below shows some of the functions of the modals and their corresponding examples in sentences.

Modal Verb	Modality/Function	Example
Must	obligation	You *must* do it.
can	ability	I *can* drive a car.
could	possibility	It *could* rain today.

will	certainty	Chelsea *will* win the match.
would	request	*Would* you please stand up?
may	prayer	*May* we succeed.
might	probability	My boss *might* travel to Abuja tomorrow.
shall	suggestion	*Shall* I switch on the fan?
should	necessity	A doctor *should* diagnose his patients.
had better	advice	They *had better* go home in time.

Dada (2017, p. 71) gave a summary of the various uses of the most common of these modals in the table below. Note that a tick (√) indicates the applicability of a function to a modal verb.

Table 1: Stylistic Continuum of Modal Auxiliary Verbs

SN	Modal	Continuum	Obligation	Certainty	Necessity	Possibility	Ability	Probability	Permission	Request	Advice	Wish
1	must	strongest	√	√	√					√		
2	have to		√	√	√					√		
3	shall		√	√	√					√	√	√
4	should		√	√	√	√				√	√	√
5	will		√	√		√				√		√
6	would		√	√		√				√		√
7	can					√	√	√	√	√	√	
8	could					√	√	√	√	√	√	
9	may					√		√	√	√	√	
10	might	weakest				√		√	√	√	√	

Source: Dada (2017, p. 71)

As the table above shows, a single modal can be used to express as many functions or uses as possible. Besides, the modals, in relation to the uses, are also in a cline, with 'must' being the strongest and 'might' being the weakest. Note also that the present tense forms of the modals are stronger than their past counterparts. This means that in expressing permission, for instance, 'can' is stronger than 'could', and 'may' than 'might' such that, among the four, 'can' is the strongest while might is the weakest. The four could, therefore, be seen as variants of the modals used in expressing permission. However, 'can' and 'could' are closer in relationship than 'may' and 'might' and vice versa. Those with such close relationship on the continuum, Dada (2017, p. 71) referred to as *primary variants* while those that are not so closely related he called *secondary variants*. The affinity which exists among the modals in performing their functions is the reason why he called them *stylistic variants*. We shall exemplify this with the following sentences.

a. You *can* sit down.

b. You *could* sit down.

c. You *may* sit down.

d. You *might* sit down.

All the above sentences express permission but in varying degrees. Sentence (a) with 'can' expresses the strongest willingness to permit the listener to sit down. This permission decreases in degree as we move towards sentence (d) with 'might' which expresses the weakest permission.

It should be noted, however, that the table above is not exhaustive of all the possible functions performed by the modals. Neither is it exhaustive, of course, of the list of the modals themselves. The aim of it is mainly to juxtapose the commonest of these verbs with their commonest uses.

Notes on the Uses of some Modal Verbs

- When 'can' is used to mean 'able to,' do not combine it with the adjective 'able' because doing so will be tautological.

  Dayo *can* read. OR Dayo *is able to* read. NOT *Dayo *can be able to* read.

  Sandra *couldn't* cook at age twelve. OR Sandra *wasn't able to* cook at age twelve. NOT *Sandra *couldn't be able to* cook at age twelve.

- If something is not compulsory, say 'need not', 'do not need to' or 'do not have to' (NOT 'must not').

  The girl *need not* come now. OR The girl *doesn't have to* come now. (NOT *The girl *must not* come now.)

  Note that the sentence in brackets looks like a threat against the girl but this is not the intention of the speaker.

- Also, note the use of 'need', in the first sentence above, not 'needs'. This use of 'need' as a modal verb is different from when it is used as a lexical verb in which case, 's' may be added, as in the sentence below:

  Everyone *needs* food and water to survive.

- Finally, the modal verb 'dare' can also be a lexical verb. When it is used as a modal verb, the 's' inflection is not needed as in: He *dare* not call me by my first name.

  But when it is used as a lexical verb, meaning to challenge someone, the 's' inflection is used e.g. He *dares* me to a fight.

4. **Finite and Non-Finite Verbs:** A finite verb is one in which person, number and tense are marked. In other words, a finite verb indicates or is affected by the person of the subject (first, second or third person), the number

of the subject (singular or plural) and the time of an action (present or past). We can, therefore, conclude that a finite verb is affected by subject and tense. We shall demonstrate this with person, number and tense.

a. Person

I am going home.

You are going home.

She is going home.

There are three persons in English: first person (the speaker), second person (the listener) and third person (someone being discussed), as represented by the pronouns 'I', 'you' and 'she' in the sentences above. You would note that the choice of different persons (I, you and she) in the sentences above affects or necessitates the choice of different verbs ('am', 'are', and 'is' respectively). Since 'am', 'are' and 'is' are forms of the verb 'be', we can conclude that the verb 'be' is a finite verb in these sentences.

b. Number

The *baby* sleeps well.

The *babies* sleep well.

In English, a subject is either singular or plural, as we have of 'baby' and 'babies' in the sentences above. The use of the singular 'baby' in the first sentence necessitates the use of the singular verb 'sleeps' while in the second sentence, the choice of the plural 'babies' warrants the choice of the plural verb 'sleep'. This makes the verb 'sleep' a finite verb here.

c. Tense

Tokunbo *gives* me money. (present)

Tokunbo *gave* me money. (past)

Tokunbo *has given* me money. (present perfect)

Tokunbo *was giving* me money. (past progressive)

From the examples above, it is clear that the different times that actions take place (tenses) influence the forms of the verb used. In the present tense, 'gives' is used; in the past, it is 'gave'; 'given' is used in the present perfect tense while 'giving' is used in the past progressive tense. This means that the verb 'give' is a finite verb in this context.

Non-finite verbs, on the other hand, are not limited or affected by person, number and tense. We shall classify them into three: infinitival, gerundial and participial non-finite verbs.

a. **Infinitival non-finite verbs** are introduced by 'to' e.g. to go, to take, to sit, etc as in: Tell him *to sit*. I want *to go*.

b. **Gerundial non-finite verbs** end in 'ing' e.g. making, bathing, sitting, going, cooking, etc as in Ann likes *cooking*. *Running* is my hobby.

Note that these sentences are different from 'Ann is cooking' and 'I am running' where 'cooking' and 'running' are finite verbs.

c. **Participial non-finite verbs** behave like past participles e.g. taken, written, gone, killed, depressed, etc.

Depressed by the death of her son, she cried all day.

Having written the letter, Emeka posted it.

Convicted, the robber pleaded for leniency.

Compare the verbs in the sentences above with the following, used as finite verbs.

She was *depressed* by the death of her son.

Emeka has *written* the letter.

The robber has been *convicted*.

Note: To differentiate between gerundial and participial non-finite verbs on the one hand, and finite verbs in 'ing' or 'en' form on the other hand, always look out for an auxiliary verb. The verb preceded by an auxiliary verb is a finite verb.

5. **Dynamic and Stative Verbs:** Jowitt (1991, p. 114) called these 'event verbs' and 'state verbs' respectively. Dynamic verbs are verbs that can be used in the progressive or continuous tense. That is, such verbs take the '-ing' inflection e.g. 'reading' and 'washing' in the sentences below:

Sam is *reading*.

Aminat was *washing*.

It should be noted that most English verbs are dynamic.

Stative verbs, on the other hand, are not ordinarily used in the progressive. Most stative verbs are those that denote the senses of sight, hearing, taste, feeling, smell, etc. Such verbs are generally called 'verbs of perception' and they include: see, hear, taste, feel, smell, know, understand, believe, like, hate, perceive, prefer, love, realize, think, want, etc. Relational verbs such as be, belong to, contain, equal, have, lack, matter, owe, own, possess, require, etc are also stative verbs (Quirk & Greenbaum, 1973, p. 47).

I (can) see you. NOT *I am seeing you.

He *knows* the answer. NOT *He is knowing the answer.

I *understood* the lecture. NOT *I was understanding the lecture.

Can/Do you *hear* me? NOT *Are you hearing me?

However, some of these stative verbs can be used in the progressive when they have special meaning, as we have in idioms and phrasal verbs:

We are *seeing off* our guests.

She was *feeling for* the light switch (in the dark).

   6. **Linking Verbs:** These are verbs that do not express action. A linking verb serves as a link or connective between a subject and its complement. Linking verbs are technically called 'copulas' (Quirk & Greenbaum, 1973, p. 352) and the 'be' verb with its various forms is the commonest copula in English. Others are: become, get, appear, seem, look, smell, feel, sound, taste, turn, grow, etc, as in:

Moses *is* a lawyer.

The leaf *turned* yellow.

It *feels* warm.

The food *tastes* sour.

Feranmi *appears* unhappy about it.

Linking verbs are sometimes called 'verbs of incomplete predication' (Wren & Martin, 2010, p.57) because they require a complement (noun or adjective) to express full or complete meaning. When a noun is used, it is called a 'predicative noun' but when an adjective is used, it is called a 'predicative adjective'.

   7. **Phrasal Verbs:** They are verbs that are combined with adverbs, prepositions or even both to produce a new meaning.

Verb	Adverb	Preposition	Meaning

come	(a)round		become conscious again
flare	up		become suddenly angry
take		after	resemble
fall	out	with	quarrel with
catch	up	with	move fast enough to reach
switch	off		turn off
come		across	meet by chance
go	in	for	take an exam/enter a competition
pull	through		survive an illness/succeed
win	over		convince or persuade
round	up		arrest/capture (offenders)
round	off		finish/complete an activity

The dead man *came around* after a series of prayers.

Ade *flared up* when I told him about his mistakes.

Mary Onyali *caught up with* the lady and soon outran her.

Cyril *came across* his primary school friend at the gym.

The meeting was *rounded off* at 1pm.

Note that adverbs or prepositions that are used in phrasal verbs are technically called 'particles'.

Forms of English Verbs

English verbs can have any of the following five forms or patterns as given by Quirk and Greenbaum (1973, p. 27).

Form	Symbol	Example	Use/Example
1. base form	V	take, go, play	a. Used for plural subjects: We/The boys *take* tea. b. Used for imperatives: *Take* the money. c. Used in subjunctives: God *take* us there safely. d. Used in to-infinitives: I wish *to take* photographs.
2. -s form	V-s	takes, goes, plays	3rd person singular present tense: He/The girl *takes* fruit regularly.
3. past form	$V\text{-}ed_1$/ V-ed	took, went, played	Simple past tense: Dorcas *took* an apple.
4. -ing participle	V-ing	taking, going, playing	Progressive aspect (be+V-ing): Deji is *taking* an exam.

5.	-ed participle	V-ed₂/ V-en	taken, gone played	a. Perfective aspect (have+V-ed₂): She has *taken* her drugs.
				b. Passive voice (be+V-ed₂): The exams were *taken*.

Verb, Time and Tense

Time is a universal phenomenon. In other words, time is a general concept and can be divided into three: past, present and future. However, tense is a grammatical term which refers to a form of the verb used to show time.

The tense system is a 'fairly complex' and 'controversial' system in English (Osisanwo, 2002, p. 108). For example, to some grammarians, such as the traditional grammarians and the systemic functional grammarians, verbs have forms that correspond to the three main divisions of time (past, present and future), thus giving three types of tense respectively: past tense, present tense and future tense. In fact, according to the systemic functional grammarians, from these three major tense types, there are as many as thirty-six tense forms (Halliday, 1966d as cited in Osisanwo, 2002, p. 112). This complexity is the reason why Afolayan (1977, p. 121) described tense as 'a system of systems'. To some other grammarians, such as transformational grammarians, there are only two types of tense (past and present) while the future tense is regarded as 'a modal construction' and the traditional progressive and perfective tenses are regarded merely as 'aspects' of the present and past tenses (Fakuade, 2002, pp. 76-77).

However, for our own purpose, we shall use a trado-systemic approach and, therefore, consider the present tense, the past tense and the future tense as the three main types of English tenses. A blend of traditional and systemic approaches here implies that terms in the two theories of grammar will be used in our discussion of tenses. For example, while the terms 'past tense', 'present tense' and 'future tense' are common to both theories, the terms used for the sub-divisions of each type of tense are traditional. So, instead of the thirty-six tense forms in SFG, we have twelve – four for each type of tense. Later on, as in the systemic orientation, we will discuss 'aspect' separately as a sub-system of the verb.

Meanwhile, we need to note that 'there is no direct relationship between verb forms and time' (Swan, 2005, p. 5) because it is possible for a verb in its past form to describe a present action (e.g. It is time we went home.) or an unreal or uncertain present or future events (e.g. Mum would be happy if you were here now). Also, verbs in their simple present tense or continuous tense can be used to express the future (e.g. Dad travels to Ghana next week. OR Dad is travelling to Ghana next week.) For these reasons, we may say that our definitions and uses of the tenses given below are hypothetical and are subject to context.

Present Tenses

A present tense is a verb that refers to an action in the present time. There are four of such tenses in English:

    a. Simple Present Tense: Among others, this is used:

        i. to express a habitual action e.g. I *jog* every morning.

        ii. to express general truths e.g. The earth *is* round.

iii. to express a fixed time table in the future e.g. The plane *takes* off at 10am.

b. **Present Progressive Tense:** Among others, it expresses:
   i. an action going on at the time of speaking e.g. Job is *laughing*.
   ii. an action which may not be going on at the time of speaking e.g. I am *teaching* ENG 201.

c. **Present Perfect Tense:** It is used, among others, to:
   i. show an action which started sometime in the past and continues up to the present time e.g. I *have known* her for five years. (I still know her.)
   ii. describe the effect of past events on the present e.g. I *have finished* my food. (Can I get more?)

d. **Present Perfect Progressive Tense:** This describes an action which began in the past and continues till the present time e.g. She *has been sleeping* since the journey began.

Past Tenses

A past tense generally describes an action that took place in the past. It is also of four types:

a. **Simple Past Tense:** This expresses an action that:
   i. was completed in the past with or without an adverb (phrase) of time e.g. Opeyemi *cooked* a delicious meal (last night).
   ii. a past habit e.g. He always *visited* me in school.

As earlier noted, the past tense is sometimes used to describe unreal or imagined present or future actions. Below are a few more examples of such.

I sometimes wish (that) I *was* a woman.

If I *had* a billion dollars now, I *would* buy an aeroplane.

She looks as if she *was* about to cry.

Supposing we *didn't* travel again next week, where *would* you go?

I'd rather you *came* tomorrow; I'm travelling today.

It's (high) time you *left* for school or you *would* be late.

    b. **Past Progressive Tense:** This indicates:

        i. an action going on in the past e.g. They *were singing* (all night).

        ii. a habit going on in the past e.g. She *was complaining* too often.

    c. **Past Perfect Tense:** This is also known as 'plu-perfect' and means 'past in the past' (Leech & Svartvik, 2012, p. 71) or 'earlier past' (Swan, 2005, p. 397) because it describes two actions in the past. It shows the first of two events that happened in the past, hence 'when', 'before' or 'after' is sometimes used in such a tense. The first action, which is the past perfect tense, is preceded by 'had' while the second action is simply expressed in a past tense e.g. We *had done* our homework before our friends came.

    Note that even if the sequence of actions in using the past perfect tense is not overtly stated in a sentence, it should be implied by the context of discussion, as in:

Faith: Adeogo *posted* the letter today. (Second action, implied)

Love: Yes, but he *had written* it since yesterday. (First action, stated)

d. **Past Perfect Progressive Tense:** It is used for an action which began before a certain point in the past and still continued up to that time e.g. He *had been working* in that company, when Harry was promoted manager.

Future Tenses

Future tenses generally indicate intention or prediction (Adegbija, 1998, p. 128) because they are expressions of future actions. There are various ways of talking about events in the future in English. These include the use of 'will/shall,' the 'be + going to' verb, the 'be + about to' verb, the simple present tense and the continuous tense. The future tense is also of four types:

a. **Simple Future Tense:** It is used to predict the future e.g. It *will* rain today.

Note that 'shall' is sometimes used with the first person pronoun (I or we) in British English while 'will' is almost always used with all personal pronouns in American English, to describe the future.

b. **Future Progressive Tense:** It is used to talk about an action that will be in progress at a particular time in the future e.g. I *shall be washing* my clothes (by) this time (of) tomorrow.

c. **Future Perfect Tense:** This describes an action that will be completed by a certain time in the future e.g. Tom *will have arrived* from London by then.

d. **Future Perfect Progressive Tense:** It is used for actions that will be in progress over a period of time that will end in the future e.g. The children *will have been watching* television for hours by 8pm.

Other Ways of Expressing the Future

- The 'be going to' verb is sometimes used like the simple future tense to predict the future e.g. It *is going to* rain today.
- The 'be about to' form is used to talk about immediate future e.g. Hurry up! We *are about to* leave. The bomb *is about to* explode.
- The 'be to' form is used to talk about arrangements in the future e.g. You *are to* come by 2 o'clock.

Verbs and Aspect

	Progressive Aspect	Perfective Aspect
Present	Gerald *is eating*.	Gerald *has eaten*.
Past	Gerald *was eating*.	Gerald *had eaten*.

In the table above, while the sentences in the first column express actions in progress, those in the second column express actions that have been completed. The manner in which a verb is used to express an on-going or completed action like this is known as 'aspect'. Thus, there are two kinds of aspect: the progressive aspect and the perfective aspect. The progressive aspect indicates an action in progress and it is divided into present progressive aspect and past progressive aspect. On the other hand, the perfective aspect shows that an action has been completed. It is also divided into present perfective aspect and past perfective aspect, as we have in the table above.

Sequence of Tenses in English

By rule in English, if a sentence is made up of a main clause and a subordinate clause, both clauses must be in the same tense. That is, a main clause in the present tense is followed by a subordinate clause in the present tense while a main clause in the past tense is followed by a subordinate clause in the past tense. This principle is known as 'sequence of tenses' as in the following sentences.

Present Tenses

Main Clause	Subordinate Clause
I *know*	what I *will* do.
That lady *feels*	that she *is* the most beautiful.
These students *work* hard	so that they *will* succeed.

Past Tenses

Main Clause	Subordinate Clause
He *asked*	if I *could* help.
They *thought*	that we *would* beat them.
The judge *found* out	that the accused person *was* guilty.
Gbenga *did* not know	that Shola *had* seen him.

Note that in either case above, it is the tense of the main clause that determines the tense of the subordinate clause and not the other way round. However, there are three exceptions to these rules, according to Adegbija (1998, p. 129). A main clause in past tense may be followed by a subordinate clause in present tense when:

1. the subordinate clause expresses universal truth e.g. He *showed* us that the moon *produces* light at night.
2. the subordinate clause shows comparison e.g. Dr Olajide *taught* us then better than how he *teaches* us now.
3. verbs are in quotations e.g. She *asked* 'What *is* your name?'

Verbs and Mood

Verbs are traditionally known as action words. However, there are different ways in which the actions performed by verbs are presented. That is, there are different perspectives to the actions of verbs. The way in which the action of a verb is expressed or presented is known as 'mood'. It should be noted that the mood here is different from the uses of the modal auxiliary verbs such as possibility, certainty, ability, etc that we earlier discussed. According to Wren and Martin (2010, pp. 62-64), there are three kinds of mood in English and they are as explained below.

   a. **Indicative Mood**: A verb used to make a statement, ask a question or make an assumption is in the indicative mood. Examples:

   Tomorrow *is* Thursday. (Statement)

   Are you deaf? (Question)

   If she *abuses* you, report to me. (Assumption)

   b. **Imperative Mood**: When a verb expresses a command, advice, a request or a prayer, it is said to be in the imperative mood, for example:

   Get out! (Command)

   Be honest at all times. (Advice)

   Could you please send me some money? (Request)

c. **Subjunctive Mood**: A verb in the subjunctive mood is used to express any of: a wish/prayer, a desire, a suggestion, a resolution, unreality, improbability, preference, etc. The subjunctive mood may either be in the present or in the past tense.

The Present Subjunctive expresses a wish, a prayer, a desire, a suggestion, a proposal, a motion, a recommendation, a resolution, etc as in:

I *wish* you good luck. (Wish)

(*May*) God *bless* you! (Prayer)

I *move* for the acceptance of the bill. (Motion)

We *recommend* that the culprit be sacked. (Recommendation)

The Past Subjunctive is used after:

- *wish* to show a situation that is contrary to fact e.g. She wishes she *were* a man.
- *if* to express unreality in the present e.g. If I *were* you, I would apologize.
- *as if/as though* to indicate an unreal condition e.g. He orders me about as though he *were* my boss.
- *it is time* to show that it is late e.g. It is time we *left* for work.
- *would rather* to indicate preference e.g. I would rather you *came* tomorrow.

Conjugation of Verbs

The term 'conjugation' was coined by traditional grammarians. To conjugate a verb is to show its various inflected forms to mark voice, mood, tense, number and person (Wren & Martin, 2010, p. 96; Murthy, 2012, p. 169) such that we have a paradigm of the verb. Below is the conjugation of the verb 'write'. Note that the portions in brackets are optional.

Simple Present Tense

Person	Number	Active Voice	Passive Voice
First	sg	I *write* books	Books *are written* (by me).
Second	sg/pl	You *write* books	Books *are written* (by you).
Third	sg	He *writes* books.	Books *are written* (by him).
	pl	They *write* books.	Books *are written* (by them).

Present Progressive Tense

Person	Number	Active Voice	Passive Voice
First	sg	I *am writing* books	Books *are being written* (by me).
Second	sg/pl	You *are writing* books.	Books *are being written* (by you).
Third	sg	He *is writing* books.	Books *are being written* (by him).

	pl	They *are writing* books	Books *are being written* (by them).

Present Perfect Tense

Person	Number	Active Voice	Passive Voice
First	sg	I *have written* books.	Books *have been written* (by me).
Second	sg/pl	You *have written* books.	Books *have been written* (by you).
Third	sg	He *has written* books.	Books *have been written* (by him).
	pl	They *have written* books	Books *have been written* (by them).

Present Perfect Progressive Tense

Person	Number	Active Voice	Passive Voice (Rare)
First	sg	I have been writing books.	Books have been being written (by me).
Second	sg/pl	You have been writing books.	Books have been being written (by you).
Third	sg	He has been writing books.	Books have been being written (by him).

| | pl | They have been writing books | Books have been being written (by them). |

Simple Past Tense

Person	Number	Active Voice	Passive Voice
First	sg	I wrote books	Books were written (by me).
Second	g/pl	You wrote books.	Books were written (by you).
Third	sg	He wrote books.	Books were written (by him).
	pl	They wrote books.	Books were written (by them).

Past Progressive Tense

Person	Number	Active Voice	Passive Voice
First	sg	I *was writing* books.	Books *were being written* (by me).
Second	sg/pl	You *were writing* books.	Books *were being written* (by you).
Third	sg	He *was writing* books.	Books *were being written* (by him).

	pl	They *were* writing books.	Books *were being written* (by them).

Past Perfect Tense

Person	Number	Active Voice	Passive Voice
First	sg	I had written books.	Books had been written (by me)
Second	sg/pl	You had written books.	Books had been written (by you)
Third	sg	He had written books.	Books had been written (by him)
	pl	They had written books.	Books had been written (by them)

Past Perfect Progressive Tense

Person	Number	Active Voice	Passive Voice (Rare)
First	sg	I *had been writing* books.	Books had been being written (by me).
Second	sg/pl.	You *had been writing* books.	Books had been being

Person	Number	Active Voice	Passive Voice
			written (by you).
Third	sg	He *had been writing* books.	Books had been being written (by him).
	pl	They *had been writing* books.	Books had been being written (by them).

Simple Future Tense

Person	Number	Active Voice	Passive Voice
First	sg	I *will write* books.	Books *will be written* (by me).
Second	sg/pl	You *will write* books.	Books *will be written* (by you).
Third	sg	He *will write* books.	Books *will be written* (by him).
	pl	They *will write* books.	Books *will be written* (by them).

Future Progressive Tense

Person	Number	Active Voice	Passive Voice (Rare)
First	sg	I *will be writing* books.	Books will be being written (by me).
Second	sg/pl	You *will be writing* books.	Books will be being written (by you).
Third	sg	He *will be writing* books.	Books will be being written (by him).
	pl	They *will be writing* books.	Books will be being written (by them).

Future Perfect Tense

Person	Number	Active Voice	Passive Voice
First	sg	I will *have written* books.	Books *will have been written* (by me).
Second	sg/pl	You *will have written* books.	Books *will have been written* (by you).
Third	sg	He *will have written* books.	Books *will have been written* (by him).
	pl	They *will have written* books.	Books *will have been written* (by them).

Future Perfect Progressive Tense

Person	Number	Active Voice	Passive Voice (Rare)
First	sg	I *will have been writing* books	Books will have been being written (by me).
Second	sg/pl	You *will have been writing* books.	Books will have been being written (by you).
Third	sg	He *will have been writing* books.	Books will have been being written (by him).
	pl	They *will have been writing* books	Books will have been being written (by them).

Note the past tenses and past participles of the following commonly problematic verbs.

Present Tense	Past Tense	Past Participle
hang (kill sb)	hanged	hanged
hang (sth)	hung	hung

lie (to sb)	lied	lied
lie (down)	lay	lain
lay (a bed, etc)	laid	laid
find (sth lost)	found	found
found (start sth)	founded	founded
grind	ground	ground
fall (down)	fell	fallen
fell (a tree)	felled	felled

Let us illustrate with one of the verbs: 'grind': She bought some ground (not *'grinded') pepper from the market. The verb 'bind' behaves the same way: I have bound (not *'binded') my final project.

Revision Exercise 5

1. List any four qualities of verbs that you have read about.
2. Write a note on any four of the following categories of verbs:
   a. Regular and Irregular Verbs
   b. Transitive, Intransitive and Ergative Verbs
   c. Lexical and Auxiliary Verbs
   d. Finite and Non-finite Verbs
   e. Dynamic and Stative Verbs
3. Use the following phrasal verbs in sentences: account for, back out, call off, catch up with, come across, fall back on, give in, give up, get through, let down, pull through, round up, round off, run into, run down, see off, see through, take off, win over, wise up.

4. Identify the five forms of English verbs with two examples each.
5. Change the following verbs to their various forms in the present, past and future tenses: be, see, fell (a tree), found (start), hang (sb), bind, have, lie (down), lay (eggs), shut.
6. What is conjugation? Conjugate the verb 'take'.

3.2.4 Adverbs

Adverbs are words which modify verbs, adjectives, prepositions, nouns and other adverbs. From this definition, it is obvious that adverbs modify/qualify most of the other parts of speech or classes of words. The majority of adverbs are easy to recognize because they have special endings. For instance, adverbs formed from adjectives end in 'ly' (correctly, slowly, angrily, wisely, etc); those that show direction end in 'wards' (inwards, backwards, southwards, etc); others express manner or viewpoint and end in 'wise' (likewise, clockwise, businesswise, etc). Some, however, have no special ending. They include often, always, early, soon, now, yet, then, very, quite, how, not, too, etc.

Features of Adverbs

a. The most striking feature of most adverbs is their derivational endings/suffixes: -ly, -wards, -wise, as in badly, southwards, clockwise respectively.
b. Some adverbs also have comparative inflectional endings such as -er, -est as in sooner and hardest respectively.
c. Most adverbs are formed from adjectives with the 'ly' derivational suffix.

Note, however, that the following words with 'ly' endings are adjectives, not adverbs: timely, deadly, friendly, cowardly, lovely, scholarly, miserly, rascally and godly. Hence, we say:

  i. a *friendly* animal

  ii. a *cowardly* soldier

  iii. a *miserly* rich woman

'Manner' is normally used with such adjectives to form adverbial phrases with them, as in: He relates with me *in a friendly manner*.

  d. Most adverbs are mobile i.e. they can be used at initial, medial or final position in a sentence, as italicized in the sentences below.

  i. *Moreover*, most adverbs are moble. (initial)

  ii. Most adverbs are, *moreover*, mobile. (medial)

  iii. Most adverbs are mobile, *moreover*. (final)

Types of Adverbs

Quirk and Greenbaum (1973, pp. 207-208) classified adverbs into three: adjuncts, disjuncts and conjuncts.

  a. **Adjuncts:** These are adverbs that are integrated into the structure of the clause (Quirk & Greenbaum, 1973). Adjuncts usually show where, when, why, how, to what extent or how often an event takes place and are thus named according to these functions.

Types of Adjuncts

  i. **Place Adjuncts** (adverbs of place) answer the question 'where?' e.g. here, there, up, down, out, away, etc.

ii. **Reason Adjuncts** (adverbs of reason) answer the question 'why?' e.g. because, for, why, therefore, hence, thus, etc.

iii. **Time Adjuncts** (adverbs of time) answer the question 'when?' e.g. now, later, then, yesterday, today, ago, soon, always, afterwards, etc.

iv. **Manner Adjuncts** (adverbs of manner) answer the question 'how?' e.g. quietly, interestingly, greatly, hard, like, etc.

v. **Intensifiers** (adverbs of degree) show how much e.g. almost, as, too, so, very, quite, etc.

vi. Note: Use 'too' with 'to' and 'so' with 'that' e.g. The patient is *too* weak *to* stand. The food was *so* tasty *that* he asked for more.

vii. **Frequency Adjuncts** (adverbs of frequency) show how often e.g. often, occasionally, always, twice, frequently, hardly, scarcely, etc.

Note: 'Thrice' is not an English word. Use 'three times' instead e.g. He sat SSCE three times.

Use 'when' with 'scarcely' and 'hardly' but 'than' with 'sooner' to show that one event started immediately after another e.g. *Hardly* had the clouds gathered *when* the 'rain' started. *No sooner* had the clouds gathered *than* the rain started.

b. **Disjuncts:** Disjuncts are peripheral to the structure of the clause (Quirk & Greenbaum, 1973). They usually express comments, emotional reactions, judgement or a speaker's attitude. Also, they usually come first in sentences and are usually marked off from the sentence with a comma. Examples of disjuncts include frankly, surprisingly, amazingly, regrettably, fortunately, wisely, interestingly, seriously, personally, sincerely, etc. e.g. Fortunately, I passed my exams.

    c. **Conjuncts:** These adverbs, like disjuncts, are peripheral to the clause. In addition, they perform connective functions or act as links between clauses or sentences. Examples of conjuncts are: meanwhile, however, similarly, first(ly), second(ly), furthermore, moreover, although, likewise, equally, consequently, otherwise, alternatively, finally, etc. Conjuncts are otherwise called *transitional markers* or *linking devices* in English.

Functions of Adverbs

Adverbs are used primarily to modify/qualify verbs but they can also modify other word classes, as explained below. Note, in this section, that the adverbs are underlined while the words they modify are in italics.

    a. Adverbs modifying verbs

        The queen *walks* majestically.

        He *speaks* clearly.

        The cheetah *runs* fast.

    b. Adverbs modifying adjectives

        Water is very *important* for living.

        The woman is extremely *beautiful*.

        This boy is more *intelligent* than that girl.

    c. Adverb modifying prepositions

        She sat right *beside* her husband.

        The train was dead *on time*.

d. Adverb modifying nouns
   I have never seen <u>such</u> *love*.
   The work was <u>rather</u> *a mess*.
   e. Adverbs modifying pronouns.
   <u>Almost</u> *everybody* liked him.
   <u>Nearly</u> *all* were present.
   I have <u>hardly</u> *any* left.
   f. Adverbs modifying other adverbs
   You write <u>too</u> *slowly*.
   God loves me <u>so</u> *very* much.
   Wale works <u>quite</u> *hard*.

Comparison of Adverbs

Just like adjectives, adverbs can be compared, and have three degrees of comparison. However, unlike adjectives, not many adverbs are comparable. For instance, a good number of the adjuncts (such as now, yesterday, here, etc and all conjuncts are incomparable. The two ways of comparing adverbs are:

   a. By adding 'er' and 'est' to the simple form (called positive) of an adverb to form its comparative and superlative degrees respectively.

Positive	Comparative	Superlative
fast	faster	fastest
late	later	latest
soon	sooner	soonest
hard	harder	hardest

It should be noted, as with the adjectives, that while the positives are used when a singular thing is involved, the comparatives are used to compare two things and the superlatives are used for three or more things.

The plane arrived *late*.

Today's plane arrived *later* than that of yesterday.

That of last week arrived the *latest* of the three planes.

  b. By placing 'more' and 'most' before the comparatives and the superlatives respectively. Adverbs that end in 'ly' are compared this way.

quickly	more quickly	most quickly
brilliantly	more brilliantly	most brilliantly
happily	more happily	most happily
successfully	more successfully	most successfully
skilfully	more skilfully	most skilfully

King Saul ruled *successfully*.

King David ruled *more successfully* than King Saul.

King Solomon ruled the *most successfully* out of the three kings.

Adverbs that take er/est or more/most as those in (a) and (b) above, are regular adverbs.

  c. However, there are irregular adverbs that are compared in a variety of ways other than those described above.

badly	worse	worst
well	better	best
little	less	least
far	farther/ further	farthest/ furthest

Fatima behaves *maturely*.

Mariam behaves *more maturely* than Fatima.

Aisha behaves the *most maturely* of all the girls in the class.

Revision Exercise 6

1. State any three attributes of adverbs.
2. What is an adjunct? Explain any five types of adjunct with five examples each.
3. Differentiate between conjuncts and disjuncts. Give five examples of each type in sentences.
4. Identify the functions of the italicized adverbs in these sentences.

   a. Ade is *more* brilliant than his sister.

   b. Evelyn writes *very* slowly.

   c. The exam started *right* on time.

   d. *Almost* all have arrived for the party.

   e. All the library users were warned to read *silently*.

Chapter Four

THE WORD: THE CLOSED CLASS

4.1 The Closed Class

The closed class or 'closed system' (Quirk & Greenbaum, 1973 p. 19) is the group of minor word classes or parts of speech such as pronouns, prepositions, conjunctions, interjections and determiners in English. The class is said to be closed because its 'membership is limited in number, and they can be listed' (Leech & Svartvik, 2012, p. 417). This means that the classes of words found here cannot be expanded by the creation or invention of new words. For example, all English pronouns can be listed and no other pronoun can be formed apart from those that we already know. Closed-class words are also known as 'grammatical' or 'function' words (Akmajian, Demers, Farmer & Harnish, 2010, p. 22).

Like the open class, we can see the closed class from two different perspectives. The first one borders on the five word classes here as a group of those with limited lexical items while the second view considers each word class as a closed class because its lexical items can be numbered. As such, the five classes of words make five closed classes. They are explained in turn as follows.

4.1.1 Pronouns

Pronouns are commonly defined as words used instead of nouns. They are, therefore, noun substitutes. Pronouns are used for co-referential purposes. A noun which has already been mentioned and to which a pronoun refers is called 'antecedent'.

Features of Pronouns

Quirk and Greenbaum (1973, p. 100) gave the following characteristics of English pronouns.

i. They do not admit determiners.
ii. They often have an objective case.
iii. They often have person distinction.
iv. They often have overt gender contrast.
v. Their singular and plural forms are often not morphologically related.

Types of Pronouns

1. **Personal Pronouns:** There are three kinds of person in English. They are:

   First person: The speaker.

   Second person: The person spoken to or the listener.

   Third person: The person spoken about.

The pronouns used in place of these persons are known as personal pronouns.

Person	Singular		Plural		Example
	Subject	Object	Subject	Object	
First	I	me	we	us	*I* can run.

Second	you	you	you	you	*You* did it.
Third	he	him	they	them	Warn *him*.
	she	her	they	them	Where's *she*?
	it	it	they	them	I know *them*.

See the section on 'Errors Relating to the Use of Pronouns' for more on the use of the subject and object personal pronouns.

Special Uses of Personal Pronouns

Note the following special uses of the personal pronouns, according to Aremo (2010, pp. 16-17), some of which have already been discussed under the heading 'Gender Category in Nouns'.

- **We** may be used (instead of 'I') by a ruler (e.g. a king or the president of a nation) to refer to himself or herself alone. This is called *the royal 'we'*. Example:
- *We* lead with the fear of God and by example.
- **We** may be used by a speaker or writer (in place of 'I'), to refer to himself or herself alone in order to avoid sounding proud:
- In chapter 2, *we* mentioned that … (i.e. In chapter 2, *I* mentioned that…)
- **We** may also be used by a speaker or writer (instead of 'you') to avoid sounding authoritative:
- So far, *we* have learnt that … (i.e. So far, *you* have learnt that …)
- **He** or **she** may be used instead of 'it' in reference to an animal (a pet) that one is interested in:

- If Jack (a dog) barks, *he* must have seen something strange.
- **She** is normally used (in place of 'it') to refer to a ship or boat or some other object that one wishes to treat with affection:
- The ship sails tomorrow morning and *she* arrives Lagos by evening.
- **It** may be used (in place of 'he' or 'she') in reference to a baby or a little child whose sex is not known or which one considers of no interest.

  The baby cries whenever *it* wants to eat or sleep.

2. **Possessive Pronouns:** These are pronouns that show ownership, as we have in the table below.

Pronoun	Meaning	Example
mine	my own	The money is *mine*.
yours	your own	This book is *yours*.
his	his own	Is the chair *his*?
Hers	her own	*Hers* is on the table.
its	its own	That tail is *its*.
ours	our own	Give us *ours*.
theirs	their own	*Theirs* has been stolen.

3. **Demonstrative Pronouns:** They are used to identify things and they can be singular or plural.

Singular	Plural	Usage
this	these	For close things
that	those	For distant things

This is my computer.

Are *these* your children?

How much is *that*?

Those were my classmates.

4. **Relative Pronouns:** A relative pronoun introduces a relative dependent clause and relates or refers to its antecedent in an independent clause. Relative pronouns in English are: who, whom, whose, that and which. Others are where, when and why (Swan, 2005, p. 479), as explained below:

- 'Who' is used for persons only and may be singular or plural. It is the nominative (subject) case of 'whom'.
- The boy *who* found the money was rewarded. ('Who' relates to 'the boy'.)
- 'Whom' is also used for persons, may be singular or plural and it is the accusative (object) case of 'who' e.g.
- The children *whom* he christened are now adults. ('Whom' relates to 'the children'.)
- 'Whose' is the genitive (possessive) case of 'who' and it is normally used for persons e.g.
- I wonder *whose* the car is. ('Whose' relates to 'the car'.)
- 'That' is used generally for nouns and it may be used for either singular or plural nouns.

  There is the girl that I told you of. ('That' relates to 'the girl' – singular.)

The phones that he bought have broken down. ('That' relates to 'the phones' – plural.)

- 'Which' is used in reference to animals, things and, sometimes, persons.

  The cows *which* were lost have been found. (animal)

  One of the windows *which* he mounted has fallen down? (thing)

  Please, tell me *which* of the candidates won the prize. (person)

- 'When' relates to antecedent nouns which refer to time, and means 'in/on/at which' (preposition + which).

  I can never forget the day *when* I got married.

- 'Where' relates to antecedent nouns referring to place and means 'in/on/at which' (preposition + which)

  Take me to the place *where* Moses was buried.

- 'Why' relates to antecedent nouns about reasons.

  Tell me the reason *why* you should not be punished.

5. **Interrogative Pronouns:** When any of the relative pronouns discussed above is used in asking a question, it automatically becomes an interrogative pronoun. Therefore, an interrogative pronoun is a pronoun used in asking questions. They are who, whose, which, when, where, why, how, what, etc.

What are you doing?

Which of the biros writes best?

Who told you about me?

How old are you?

Why is she crying?

6. **Indefinite Pronouns:** Indefinite pronouns make reference to nouns in a general way. They include: one, none, all, some, any, few, a few, most, little, a little, much, many. Others formed from a combination of 'some', 'any', 'no' and 'every' are:

some: somebody, someone, something

any: anybody, anyone, anything

no: nobody, no one, nothing

every: everybody, everyone, everything

One should take care of one's health.

All on board the plane died in the crash.

Give me *some* of the honey.

Nothing is too difficult for God to do.

Note that in British English, 'one' is followed by 'one's' as in the first example above, while in American English, it is followed by 'his' or 'her' thus: 'One should take care of his/her health.

Also, note that a singular verb is used with the compound forms of 'every' e.g.

Everybody *knows* my name.

7. **Reflexive Pronouns:** These are pronouns used to show that the subject of a verb is also the object of the same verb. In other words, the subject is the victim of its own action or there is a boomerang of action. The reflexive pronouns are formed from personal pronouns such as 'me', 'you', 'him' and 'it' and they may be singular or plural.

Singular	Plural
myself	ourselves
yourself	yourselves
himself	themselves
herself	themselves
itself	themselves

While peeling an orange, Jide cut *himself*.

I bit *myself* when eating.

We can teach *ourselves* syntax.

The dog saw *itself* in the stream.

8. **Emphatic Pronouns:** These are pronouns used for the purpose of emphasis and, like the reflexive pronouns, they may be singular or plural.

She *herself* did the work. ('Herself' emphasizes 'she'.)

Dr Carson *himself* performed the surgery. ('Himself' emphasizes 'Dr Carson'.)

The guests met the governor *himself*. ('Himself' emphasizing 'the governor'.)

9. **Reciprocal Pronouns:** They are pronouns used to show mutual or shared relationship between nouns. They are: each other, one another.

Romeo and Juliet loved *each other*. (Romeo loved Juliet and Juliet loved Romeo too.)

The children fought *one another*. (Each child fought the other.)

Note: Contrary to the misconception in some quarters that 'each other' is used with only two persons or things and 'one another' with three or more, 'Each other and one another mean the same'(Swan, 2005, p. 153). Hence, the two pronouns can be used interchangeably with either two or more persons or things. However, note the following difference in meaning between 'each other'/'one another' and 'themselves'.

- **a.** 'The husband and wife love each other/one another' means the husband loves his wife and the wife loves her husband also.)
- **b.** 'The husband and wife love themselves' means the husband loves only himself and the wife also loves only herself.
10. **Distributive Pronouns:** They are pronouns that refer to individual persons or things. They are always singular and must be followed by singular verbs. Distributive pronouns in English are 'each', 'either' and 'neither'.

Each of the workers was paid fully.

Call me *either* of the two men.

Neither of the answers is correct.

'Either' means 'one or the other of two' while 'neither' means 'not one nor the other of two' (Wren & Martin, 2010, p.43). Therefore, both 'either' and 'neither' are usually about two things only. When more than two things are involved, 'any', 'no one' or 'none' should be used, as in:

Any of the twenty-four runners can win the marathon.

Case Category in Pronouns

Just like we have with nouns, pronouns have three main types of case in English.

a. **Nominative Case**: This refers to pronouns functioning as subject (doer) of a verb (an action) e.g. *He* taught us English. *They* are eating.

b. **Accusative Case**: This refers to the function of pronouns as direct object (receiver) of a verb (an action) e.g. An ant bit *her*. Kindly call *them* for me.

c. **Genitive Case**: A pronoun is in genitive case when it shows ownership e.g. Is the dress *hers*? The house is *mine*. *Whose* is that car?

The table below shows pronouns in the three cases.

Nominative Case	Accusative Case	Genitive Case
I	me	mine
you	you	yours
he	him	his
she	her	hers
it	it	its
they	them	theirs
who	whom	whose

Functions of Pronouns

Since pronouns are substitutes for nouns, they perform the same functions as nouns, such as:

i. Subject of a verb

He took the keys. ('He' as subject of the verb 'took')

ii. Direct object of a verb

We have given *it* to the owner. ('It' as direct object of the verb 'given')

iii. Indirect object of a verb

The nurse gave *her* an injection. ('Her' as indirect object of the verb 'gave')

iv. Complement of a subject.

Who are *you*? ('You' as complement of the subject 'who')

Revision Exercise 7

1. Identify any four attributes of pronouns that you have read about in this book.
2. Describe any six kinds of pronouns in English. Give five examples of each.
3. What case is the italicized pronoun in each of the following sentences in?
   a. That pen is *mine*.
   b. *Yours* has a red cover.
   c. Donald beat *them*.
   d. *Nobody* is perfect; only God is.
   e. Whose children are *those*?
4. State any four functions of pronouns and back up each function with a sentential example.

4.1.2 Prepositions

A preposition is a word which 'expresses a relationship between two entities' (Quirk & Greenbaum, 1973, p. 143). The two grammatical entities are a noun or pronoun and a prepositional complement. A prepositional complement (PC) is normally a noun (phrase) but it may also be an adverb, an adjective, a prepositional phrase or even a clause, as in the examples below. Note that the prepositions are underlined while their complements are italicized.

    i. <u>At</u> (the) *worst*, Kayode will score 50% in the exam. (noun as PC)

    ii. The goat jumped <u>over</u> *the fence*. (noun phrase as PC)

    iii. I will see you <u>before</u> *long*. (adverb as PC)

    iv. She came <u>from</u> *inside the room*. (prepositional phrase as PC)

    v. Tunji was punished <u>for</u> *what he did*. (noun clause as PC)

Features of Prepositions

1. They usually appear before nouns/noun phrases and pronouns e.g. *at* the airport, *in* the war, *for* us, *to* me, etc.
2. Prepositions can introduce prepositional phrases as well as adjectival phrases. In the examples below, the prepositions are underlined while the phrases they introduce (their complements) are italicized.

Prepositional Phrases Adjectival Phrases

The lady is <u>from</u> *America*. The lady <u>from</u> *America* is tall.

She is <u>in</u> *a gown*. Where is the woman <u>in</u> *a gown*?

3. Prepositions do not accept inflection or affixes.
4. They are exhaustible because they can all be listed.

Types of Prepositions

    a. Simple prepositions consist of single words such as: at, to, in, on, of, up, by, off, for, from, down, over, with, past, about, along, since, after, under, until, above, below, before, beside, around, through, between, throughout, etc.

  b. **Compound prepositions** are those that comprise two or more words and they can be rightly called prepositional phrases. They are of the following structures:

- Adv/Adj/Conj/Prep + Prep: owing to, due to, because of, away from, out of, up to, as for, according to, instead of, along with.

- Prep + Noun (phrase) + Prep: by means of, in addition to, in comparison with, in front of, as a result of, in the light of, by way of, on account of, in accordance with, in place of, with regard to, in view of, on behalf of, in case of, in the event of, etc.

The following are some compound prepositions used in sentences:

i. The man died *on account of* ill health.

ii. *In addition to* teaching, he also enjoys farming.

iii. I apologize, *on behalf of* the union, for starting the meeting late.

iv. *In the event of* another robbery, call the police.

v. The culprit behaves like a fish *out of* water.

vi. It is *up to* you to decide on what to do.

vii. *As for* me and my family, we will serve the Lord.

Relationships Expressed by Prepositions

1. **Place**: Some prepositions are used to show that a relationship of place exists between the entities they describe. Such prepositions are: about, across, against, at,

in, behind, before, beside, after, over, round, under, between, within, in front of, etc.

Children are playing *under* the tree.

Run *across* the road.

Lean *against* the fence.

2. **Time**: Certain prepositions show relation of time. They include: at, before, after, during, since, from, throughout, until, by, for, about, in, between, etc.

   Come *before* evening.

   We have been waiting *since* 10a.m.

   The bus arrived *at* 7 o'clock.

   I'll see you *in* the afternoon.

3. **Instrumentality**: This is when a preposition is used to show what is used to achieve a purpose. Such prepositions are by, with, through, with the aid of, by means of, etc.

   With the aid of a labeled diagram, show the human digestive system.

   Samson killed a lion *with* bare hands.

   I go to school *by* car.

4. **Cause/Reason**: Some other propositions show what is responsible for or the reason for something. They include for, because of, for the good of, to, on account of, etc.

   She lost her job *on account of* negligence.

   They lost him *to* cancer.

5. **Contrast/Concession**: When a preposition shows that despite what has happened, a condition is still (not) met, such a preposition is one of contrast or concession. They include in spite of, after, for, despite, etc.

   With all his money, he is not happy.

   For every kobo he lost, he made a naira in return.

   He failed the test *in spite of* all his efforts.

Prepositions and Collocation

Collocation is linguistic co-occurrence i.e. the tendency for some expressions to co-occur or be used together. Particular prepositions are commonly used with some words, as in the list below:

Note: sb = somebody; sth = something

   a. **Words that commonly take the preposition *for* after them**: famous, remarkable, cure, affection, apologize (sth), appetite, notorious, affection, known, blame, capacity, admiration, compassion, compensation, desire, fondness, esteem, leisure, liking, match, need, passion, pretext, sorry, remorseful, reputation, anxious, designated, ready, sufficient, useful, zealous, destined, fit, good, qualified, grateful, prepared, eligible, desperate, etc.

   b. **Words that commonly take the preposition *to* after them**: allergic, averse, indebted, confined, complain (sb), used, accustomed, susceptible, resort, due, hostile, access, allegiance, peculiar, alternative, antidote, relevant, approach, insensitive, limited, indifferent, invitation, key, obedience, yield, objection, opposition, preface, apologize (sb), agree (sth), assent, consent, prone, conducive, resort, subject, equal, succumb, tantamount, attribute, superior, prefer, inimical, reference, repugnant, similar, sequel, indigenous, submission, supplement, etc.

c. **Words that commonly take the preposition *in* after them**: originate, absorbed, backward, deficient, experienced, diligent, shoot (sb), disappointed (sb), interested, involve, versed, intervene, acquiesce, dabble, enlist, excel, delight, indulge, confident (sb), confide, invest, result, stab, etc.

d. **Words that commonly take the preposition *with* after them**: associated, endowed, agree (sb), argue (sb), charge, acquainted, quarrel (sb), diagnose (sb), intercourse, bargain, alliance, compare, conversant, delighted, gifted, infatuated, infected, connive, inspire, overcome, replete, satisfied, interfere, bear, clash, coincide, cope, dispense, fill, comply, condole, sympathise, part, credit, experiment, conspire, etc.

e. **Words that commonly take the preposition *of* after them**: enemy, assure, proof, result, acquit, beware, boast, complain (sth), afraid, devoid, certain, cautious, characteristic, composed, conscious, confident (sth), die, approve, dispose, dream, heal, repent, sure, etc.

f. **Words that commonly take the preposition *from* after them**: abstain, secede, deliver, digress, deviate, escape, exempt, come, different, exclude, prevent, protect, prohibit, recover, refrain, desist, emerge, preserve, cease, alight, derive, etc.

g. **Words that commonly take the preposition *at* after them**: good, expert, surprised, throw, shoot, shout, bark, etc.

h. **Words that commonly take the preposition *on* after them**: rely, depend, comment, advise, decide, deliberate, dwell, embark, encroach, impose, insist, intrude, trample, conclude, argue, agree, etc.

Functions of Prepositions

1. Prepositions function as heads of prepositional phrases e.g. in the prepositional phrases '*during* harmattan' and '*in* the garden', the prepositions 'during' and 'in' function as heads of the phrases.

2. They also function as particles in phrasal verbs, for instance, in the phrasal verbs 'take after', 'pass on', 'look up' and 'take over', the prepositions 'after', 'on', 'up', and 'over' function as particles.

Revision Exercise 8

1. What is a prepositional complement? With suitable examples, discuss the structure of the prepositional complement.

2. Differentiate between simple prepositions and compound prepositions. Examine the structure of compound prepositions.

3. Explain and illustrate any four relationships which prepositions are used to express.

4. Give any three features of prepositions.

5. Complete the following sentences with the right prepositions.

    a. Akin was charged ... forgery and impersonation.

    b. She met her husband ... a bus en route to Ilorin.

c. In the past, our ancestors travelled across nations ... foot.

d. Her constant lateness to work is tantamount ... negligence of duty.

e. The superiority of this fabric ... that is obvious.

f. Do you truly prefer a bungalow ... a duplex?

g. My father is very good ... music.

h. Two of my friends work ... NNPC.

Choose from the given options to answer questions (i) and (j).

i. What are you discussing/discussing about?

j. The company has *ordered for/ordered* another fleet of cars.

4.1.3 Conjunctions

Examine these sentences:

a. Yvonne *and* Rita are intimate friends.

b. Stop the noise *or* you will be punished.

c. It rained heavily *yet* he did not wake up.

d. Hadiza succeeded *because* she worked hard.

e. *Although* he fell down, he won the race.

In (a) above, two words, 'Yvonne' and 'Allan', are joined together by 'and'. Also, in each of (b), (c), (d) and (e), two groups of words are joined together by 'or', 'yet', 'because' and 'although' respectively. Words that are used to join expressions together like these are known as conjunctions. Therefore, conjunctions are words that join words and groups of words together.

Features of Conjunctions

1. They are connectives or links within sentences.
2. Conjunctions cannot be inflected (by affixation).
3. They are of limited membership.

Types of Conjunctions

1. **Coordinating Conjunctions:** These are conjunctions used to join expressions of the same grammatical rank or status together. In other words, they join 'words of the same word class' or those of a 'similar function' (Leech & Svartvik, 2012, p. 279). Coordinating conjunctions, also called coordinators, include: and, but, or, nor, for, yet, still, else, otherwise, etc.

   Let's consider the status of the expressions (in italics) joined by the coordinators (underlined) in these sentences:

   Edward and *Joan* will soon marry. (Both are nouns.)

   The weather is *cold* but *harsh*. (Both are adjectives).

   It rained heavily yet *he did not wake up*. (Both are clauses.)

The following are the kinds of coordinators, according to Wren and Martin (2010).

   a. **Copulative Coordinators**: These are used for making addition e.g. 'and' as in 'The woman is a good wife *and* the man is a good husband'.

b. **Disjunctive Coordinators**: These are conjunctions of choice or alternative e.g. or, else, otherwise, etc as in 'Hurry up (*or*) *else* you will be late'.

c. **Adversative Coordinators**: These show contrast e.g. but, yet, still, etc as in 'The train derailed *but* there was no casualty'.

Note that it is wrong to combine 'still' and 'yet' in a sentence; only one of them should be used at a time e.g.

*The train derailed still yet there was no casualty. (Wrong)

The train derailed still/yet there was no casualty. (Right)

d. **Illative Coordinators**: They are used for making inferences e.g. as, for, etc as in 'She is alive *as* she is still breathing'.

2. **Subordinating Conjunctions**: A subordinating conjunction or a subordinator joins a subordinate or dependent clause (DC) to a main or independent clause (IC). The subordinating conjunction, therefore, usually introduces the subordinate or dependent clause in a sentence. A subordinate clause does not make full sense and always depends on the main clause for its complete meaning. There are many subordinators in English and they include: when, while, before, after, since, until, because, why, if, provided, unless, except, whether, who, whose, whom, which, that, how, although, etc as exemplified below.

I will reach home (IC) *before* it rains (DC).

He will beat you (IC) *if* you lie (DC).

Do you know (IC) *where* she hid the jewellery (DC)?

Because it was sunny (DC) he used an umbrella (IC).

Although he is wealthy (DC) he is not happy (IC).

She cursed the man (IC) *who* impregnated her (DC).

Types of Subordinating Conjunctions

Subordinating conjunctions can be classified functionally into those of:

    a. Time: when, while, since, before, after, until, etc.

    b. Place: where, etc

    c. Cause: why, because, etc.

    d. Result: so, etc.

    e. Condition: if, provided, unless, except, whether, etc.

    f. Concession: (al)though, despite, etc.

    g. Relative: that, who, whom, whose, which, etc.

    h. Manner: how, like, etc

3. **Correlative Conjunctions**, also called correlatives, are the conjunctions that are normally used in pairs to join expressions together. They are: either ... or, neither ... nor, not only ... but also, whether ... or, etc.

    Either the man *or* his wives are to blame.

    Not only is he a medical doctor *but also* a pastor.

    She does not know *whether* to marry the man *or* not.

    (See the section on 'Concord in English' for more on the use of the correlatives.)

4. **Quasi-coordinators**: This is another type of conjunctions, as suggested by Quirk and Greenbaum

(1973, p. 276). As the name implies, quasi-coordinators appear like coordinators but they are different in use. For instance, the coordinator 'and' joins together two nouns of equal status and usually requires a plural verb when used but this is not so with the quasi-coordinators. Rather, it is the first of the two nouns joined together by a quasi-coordinator that determines the choice of the verb. This is because the first noun is considered as the main subject while the second noun is merely parenthetical. Examples of quasi-coordinators are: with, together with, along with, in conjunction with, as well as, in addition to, as much as, rather than, more than, like, etc.

Food *as well as* clothes is a necessity of life.

Eight children *in addition to* one adult were victims of the flood.

The boy, *like* his three friends, has a toy car.

Note that 'quasi' is pronounced /kweizai/. (See the section on 'Concord in English' for more on the use of the quasi-coordinators.)

Functions of Conjunctions

1. Conjunctions such as 'and', 'as well as', 'not only ... but also', etc are used to express addition.
2. Conjunctions such as 'or', 'either ... or', 'otherwise', etc express choice.
3. Some conjunctions are used to show cause and effect e.g. because, therefore, as, so, since, etc.
4. Some others show time e.g. when, while, until, after, before, etc

(Source: za.pinterest.com/amp/pin/525302744007755519)

Differences between Conjunctions and Conjuncts

- Whereas, a conjunction normally links units (words, phrases and clauses) within sentences together, a conjunct normally serves as a link between paragraphs. Conjuncts engender coherence i.e. the smooth flow of our write-ups by logically linking points or paragraphs together. This is why they are called transitional devices/markers.

- Also, while conjunctions belong to the closed class of words, conjuncts belong to the open class of words.

- Finally, while the position of a conjunction is usually fixed between the units it joins, a conjunct is usually mobile. That is, a conjunct can appear or be used in any position (initial, medial or final) in a sentence but not a conjunction. Let us demonstrate this.

Conjunction

1. **But* he came I did not see him. (initial)
2. *I did not see him he came *but*. (final)
3. He came *but* I did not see him. OR I did not see him *but* he came. (medial)

Only the sentences in (3) are correct out of the above sentences because the conjunction 'but' can only function in medial position in those sentences.

Conjunct

a. *Therefore*, the students were punished. (initial)

b. The students, *therefore*, were punished. (medial)

c. The students were punished, *therefore*. (final)

All the three sentences above are correct because the conjunct 'therefore' can be used in any position in the sentences.

Revision Exercise 9

1. Write a short note on the following types of conjunction.

   a. Coordinating conjunctions

   b. Subordinating conjunctions

   c. Correlative conjunctions

2. Differentiate between coordinating conjunctions and quasi-coordinators. Use two examples of each type in two sentences.

3. Mention any three attributes of conjunctions that you have learnt about.

4. Identify any three functions of conjunctions.

5. Clearly distinguish between conjunctions and conjuncts.

4.1.4 Interjections

Interjections are sudden expressions of emotion such as joy, sadness, excitement, surprise, love, hatred, disgust, approval, etc. They are, therefore, used to express spontaneous feelings or reactions. Interjections are also called exclamations and always end with an exclamation mark (!). Examples of emotions and their corresponding interjections are:

Happiness: Hurrah! Yes! Congratulations!

Sadness: Alas! No!

Approval: Wow! Well done! Bravo! Yeah! Brilliant!
Surprise: What! Good gracious! Jesus! Oh!
Fear: Oh! Ah!
Pain: Ouch! Oh! Ah!
Appreciation: Thank you!
Warning: Watch out! Beware! Stop!
Disapproval: Idiot! No! Poor! Shut up!

Features of Interjections

1. Interjections always end with the exclamation mark (!).
2. Any word class can function as an interjection e.g. What! (pronoun), Jesus! (noun), Good! (adjective), Stop! (verb), Certainly! (adverb), etc.
3. Although they are mostly single words, they can also function as (minor) sentences e.g. Come!, Sleep!, etc.
4. Interjections are more prominent in the spoken discourse than in the written medium.
5. They are more prominently used in informal language than in formal language.

Types of Interjections

We propose the following types of interjections:

    a. **Lexical Interjections**: These are individual words used as interjections e.g. Ah! Oh! Yes! Hello! Hurray! What! Bravo! etc.

b. **Structural Interjections**: These are groups of words used as interjections e.g. Gracious God! Watch out! What a handsome boy! Don't be stupid! etc.

Functions of Interjections

1. Interjections are used to express feelings.
2. They serve as discourse markers in informal language.

Revision Exercise 10

1. Cite any six emotions expressed by interjections and one corresponding example of interjection for each case.
2. Identify four of the features of interjections.
3. State any two functions of interjections.
4. Differentiate between lexical interjections and structural interjections. Give five examples of each type.

4.1.5 Determiners

In English, determiners are words that introduce nouns and noun phrases. This means that determiners pre-modify nouns and noun phrases. In this respect, determiners function in a similar way as adjectives but they are not adjectives. The differences between determiners and adjectives are discussed at the end of this section.

Features of Determiners

1. Determiners are always followed by nouns or noun phrases.
2. Many of the determiners are derived from pronouns e.g. possessives, demonstratives, interrogatives, relatives, indefinites, quantifiers, etc.

Classes of Determiners

Determiners are broadly classified into three by Greenbaum and Nelson (2009, p. 52). Note that the names also denote their order or sequence of use i.e. pre-determiners are used before central determiners and central determiners are used before post-determiners.

1. **Pre-Determiners**: These, as the name suggests, are used before the central determiners. Pre-determiners are of the following types:

    a. **Multipliers** e.g. double, twice, three times, etc as in: double my rent, twice the president.

    b. **Fractions** e.g. half, one-third, two-fifth, etc as in: half the salary, two-third (of) the population.

    c. **Quantifiers** e.g. all, both, such, etc as in: all your children, both (the) parents, etc.

2. **Central Determiners**: This is the most important and the largest of the classes of determiners. It is sub-grouped into:

    a. **Articles:** These are of two types:

    i. Definite article: 'the' describing a specific noun e.g. the box.

    ii. Indefinite articles: 'a' and 'an' describing a non-specific or generic noun as in 'a table', 'an egg', etc.

Note that 'a' is used with a singular noun that starts with a consonant sound (not letter) while 'an' modifies a singular noun which begins with a vowel sound (not letter) as in:

A: a school, a house, a banana, a hotel, a university, a union, a European, a ewe, etc.

An: an orange, an axe, an iron, an hour, an honour, an honest man, an heir, an SSS student, etc.

    b. Demonstratives: this, these, that, those as in: this car, that house, these stones, etc.

    c. Possessives: my, our, your, his, her, its, their, whose, Anita's as in: our bicycle, its tail, Anita's bucket, etc.

    d. Interrogatives: what, which, whose as in: what time?, whose son?, etc.

    e. Relatives: which, whose, whichever, whosoever, as in: which class, whose dictionary, etc.

    f. Indefinites: some, any, no, enough, every, each, either, neither as in: some honey, no food, every child, etc.

Note that only one central determiner can be used at a time i.e. no two or more of them can be combined to modify a noun (phrase) at the same time. They are, therefore, mutually exclusive. Demonstratives, possessives, interrogatives, relatives and indefinites are derived from pronouns and they may, therefore, be called *pronominal determiners* or *derived determiners*.

    3. **Post-Determiners:** These are used after the central determiners and are divided into:

        a. Numerals: Numerals can be:

        b. Cardinal numerals such as one, two, three, etc as in *two* rivers, *six* hunters, etc.

            iii. Ordinal numerals such as first, second, third, etc as in *first* athlete, *tenth* month, etc.

a. **General Ordinals**: These include next, last, etc as in *next* person, *last* year, etc.

Note that the numerals can co-occur to introduce a noun (phrase). Examples are: *first two* years, *last three* students, etc.

b. **Quantifiers**: They are many, few, a few, little, a little, much, more, several, etc as in *many* voices, *little* oil, *several* days, etc.

Leech and Svartvik (2012, p. 50) gave the following scale of the commonest quantifiers or amount words which range from the positive inclusive 'all' at the top to the negative non-inclusive 'no' or 'none' at the bottom.

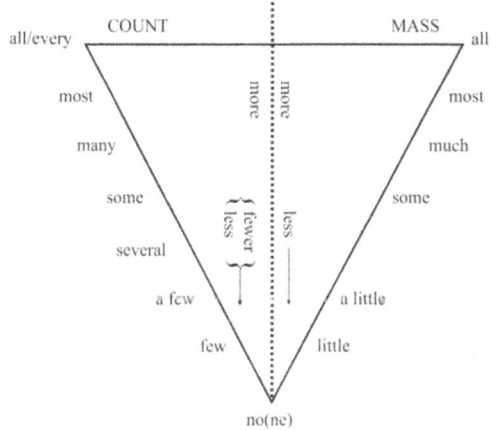

Figure 4: Scale of Amount or Quantity

Source: Leech and Svartvik (2012, p. 50)

Note that 'every', 'many', 'several', 'a few', 'few' and 'none' are used with countable nouns only; 'much', 'a little', and 'little' are used with uncountable nouns alone while 'all', 'most', 'some' and 'no' have dual roles i.e. they can be used with both. Hence, we say:

Count: *every* one of the/*many*/*several*/*a few*/*few*/*none* of the horses/ladies/schools/plants etc.

Mass: *much*/*a little*/*little* water/salt/love/joy etc.

Dual: *all*/*most*/*some*/*no* horses/ladies/schools/water/salt/love/joy etc.

Also, note that we have 'more' of a particular count noun as we move up the scale and 'fewer/less' of it as we move down it. Likewise, there is 'more' of a mass noun as we progress up the scale and 'less' of it as we move down. Finally, while 'a few' and 'a little' are used with the positive meaning of 'enough', 'few' and 'little' have the negative meaning of 'not enough'. The meaning of 'a few' and 'a little' is, therefore, closer to 'some' than that of 'few' and 'little'. Compare:

1. There are *a few* students around. (So, the lecture can start.)

   a. There are *few* students around. (So, the lecture will be postponed.)

2. Add *a little* sugar to the tea. (some)

   b. Add *little* sugar to the tea. (not much)

The quantifier 'some' is not always used with plural nouns; it can also be used with unknown or unidentified singular nouns. This way, it is similar in meaning and usage to the indefinite article 'a' or 'an' as in: *Some* person brought the letter for you.

Note on '(a) little'

The word '(a) little' can be used in various ways: as an adjective, an adverb, a determiner and a pronoun.

- When it functions as an adjective, it means, among other things, 'small' or 'young' and it is used with countable nouns only. In this sense, its comparative and superlative forms are 'littler' and 'littlest' respectively (though, rarely so used) or, more commonly, 'smaller' and 'smallest' respectively. (See Hornby, 2015) Examples:

The old woman has a *little* (small) hut up the hill.

He likes *little* (young) children.

Her baby is *littler/smaller* than yours.

That is the *littlest/smallest* hut in the village.

- When 'little' functions as an adverb, it means 'not much' and it is only used with uncountable nouns. Its comparative and superlative degrees are respectively 'less' and 'least'. Examples:

The baby only cried *a little*.

The boy cried *less* than the girl.

Maximus is the *least* scared of the men.

- As a determiner, 'little' means 'not much' and it is used with uncountable nouns only. Here, it has no comparative or superlative form, just like the other determiners. Here are some examples:

Mummy gave her *little* food.

Give me *a little* time to think about your proposal.

- Finally, as a pronoun, 'little' also means 'not much' and is only used with uncountable nouns.
I heard *little* of their conversation.

Only a *little* of the work has been done.

The phenomenon involved in the various uses of '(a) little' here is elaborately discussed under the section entitled 'The Multifunctionality of English Words' in this chapter.

Differences between Adjectives and Determiners

Both adjectives and determiners introduce or pre-modify nouns and this similarity is the reason why many students tend to interchange the two concepts. You may even see in some English grammar textbooks that the determiners are categorized as adjectives. Notwithstanding, there are clear differences between them and few of these are proposed here.

1. Adjectives belong to the open class of words while determiners belong to the closed class of words. Among other things, what this means is that while adjectives are not exhaustible, determiners are.

2. Most adjectives can be used both attributively and predicatively but most determiners can only be used attributively. Consider the positions of the adjective 'good' and the determiner 'the' in the following table.

Position	Adjective	Determiner
Attributive	He is a *good* man.	*The* man is here.
Predicative	The man is *good*.	*Man *the* is here.

3. Adjectives readily qualify both nouns and pronouns whereas determiners can only modify nouns. In the table below, the adjectives and determiners are underlined but the nouns or pronouns which they modify are italicized.

Word Class	Adjective	Determiner

Noun	I have a <u>new</u> watch	<u>My</u> *watch* cost a fortune
Pronoun	*It* is <u>new</u>	*<u>My</u> it* cost a fortune

Revision Exercise 11

1. Identify four characteristics of determiners.
2. Elaborately discuss the classes of pre-determiners and post-determiners in English with copious examples.
3. Explain any five sub-types of central determiners with two examples each.
4. Show, with a suitable diagram, the various quantifiers in English. Use each quantifier in a sentence.
5. State three differences between determiners and adjectives and cite convincing examples.
6. Complete these sentences with one of the given options.

    a. Miss Yvonne is … European woman. (a, an)

    b. Only … men are required for the job. (few/a few)

    c. … bottles were broken in the accident. (Many, Much)

    d. Raymond is … honest boy. (a, an)

    e. … baby must be vaccinated at birth. (Every/All)

4.2 The Multifunctionality of English Words

'Knowing a word means not only knowing its literal definition but also its relationship to other words, its connotations in different contexts, and its power of transformation into various other forms' (Kieffer & Lesaux, 2007, p. 136). This assertion informs the above sub-topic. It is not enough to know the function of individual English words. You should also know that a single word may have different functions based on its situation of use, also called 'context'. Consider the functions of the word 'round' in the following sentences.

    a. He was a *round* peg in a *round* hole for the task. (Adjective)

    b. The first *round* of the game was tough. (Noun)

    c. Go *round* and check the facilities yourself. (Adverb)

    d. *Round* up the score to 40. (Verb)

    e. The earth moves *round* the sun. (Preposition)

The context of a word is usually derivable from its sentence. For instance, in sentence (a) to (e) above, the same word 'round' performs different functions (adjective, noun, adverb, verb and preposition respectively). A word that can perform different roles like this is, thus, a multifunctional word. The multifunctionality of most English words is the reason why it is difficult to determine the part of speech of a word unless it is used in a sentence.

Other multifunctional words and their examples in sentences are:

1. back

    a. Harry sat in the *back* of the bus. (Noun)

    b. The electorate promised to *back* her up in the election. (Verb)

    c. Play the ball *back* to me. (Adverb)

    d. *Back* benchers are considered unserious people. (Adjective)

2. second

a. You have five more *seconds*. (Noun)
b. Tell the *second* person to come in. (Adjective)
c. I wish to *second* the motion. (Verb)
d. Kazeem came *second* in the test. (Adverb)

3. what
   a. *What* is your name? (Pronoun)
   b. Tell me *what* time to come back. (Determiner)
   c. *What*! You, of all people, failed? (Interjection)

4. right
   a. Know your *rights* and responsibilities. (Noun)
   b. Dolapo gave the *right* answer. (Adjective)
   c. Mr President has promised to *right* his wrongs. (Verb)
   d. I'll be *right* back. (Adverb)

5. like
   a. What are your *likes* and dislikes? (Noun)
   b. It's good to work with people of *like* mind. (Adjective)
   c. Do you *like* what you do? (Verb)
   d. It was, *like*, strange. (Adverb)
   e. Taiwo looks very much *like* Kehinde. (Preposition)
   f. The movie ended *like* we had anticipated. (Conjunction)

6. that
   a. How much is *that* gun? (Determiner)

b. *That* was my teacher in secondary school. (Pronoun)

c. Alice knew *that* she was right. (Conjunction)

d. The weather is not *that* cold. (Adverb)

Revision Exercise 12

1. In sentences, use each of these words in three different parts of speech. Indicate, in brackets, after each sentence, the part of speech of each word: up, well, first, good, in, some, after, quiet, fast, home.

PART TWO: SYNTAX

Chapter Five

THE PHRASE

5.1 The Concept of Phrase

a. *Felix* is a businessman.

b. She speaks *confidently*.

c. They *have been singing*.

d. His shoes are *very old indeed*.

e. The baby tore two pages *from the book*.

All the expressions in italics in the above sentences are phrases. Traditionally, phrases are groups of words such as those in (c), (d) and (e) above. But in the modern sense, a single word can also function as a phrase, as we have in (a) and (b) above. This position is corroborated by Greenbaum and Nelson (2009, p. 65) and Fakuade (2012, p. 198). Nevertheless, always remember that while a word may function as a phrase, a phrase cannot function as a word. Next to the word, up the grammatical rankscale, is the phrase. A phrase is a combination of one or more words.

Therefore, a phrase is a word or a group of words without a finite verb. (Please, see the section on verbs for explanation on finite verbs.) Phrases do not make complete sense unless they are added to other words or groups of words. This is why they are said to form part of sentences. The term 'phrase' which is a traditional category, is also known as 'group' in Systemic Functional Grammar. Hence, 'noun phrase' refers to 'noun group', 'adverbial phrase' refers to 'adverbial group', etc. However, note that the abbreviations NP, VP, AdjP, PP and AdvP, used for the phrases here, are those normally used in Transformational Generative Grammar.

5.2 Types of Phrases

5.2.1 Noun Phrases (NP)

A noun phrase is a phrase which functions as a noun. Nouns are names and so are noun phrases. Alternatively, a noun phrase is a phrase headed by a noun. Either a noun or a pronoun can serve as a noun phrase. Examples of noun phrases include:

i. boys

ii. the *boy*

iii. *boys* only

iv. one of the best *boys* in the class

The Structure of Noun Phrases

In Systemic Grammar, the most important word in a noun phrase which consists of more than one word, is called headword (h). Other words before the headword are called 'modifier' (m) while those after it are known as 'qualifier' (q). Only the headword is mandatory in a noun phrase and it is, therefore, not bracketed in the structure thus: (m) h (q). This means that a noun phrase may be made up of only the headword (as in example (i) above), modifier and headword (as in (ii) above), headword and qualifier (as in (iii) above) or a combination of the three elements – modifier, headword and qualifier – (as in (iv) above). Therefore, all the possible structures of a noun phrase are as given below.

Note: Under the structures of the phrases, the head of each phrase is italicized, when there are more than one word in the given examples, as in the following.
- headword e.g. Busayo, he, trees, love, dear, etc.
- modifier + headword e.g. the *trees*, my *love*, a live *fish*, etc.
- headword + qualifier e.g. *house* on the rock, *neighbour* next door, etc.
- modifier + headword + qualifier e.g. my *love* for you, the *food* on the fire, etc.

The table below summarizes the structure.

Modifier	Headword	Qualifier
	trees	
my	love	
	house	on the rock
my	love	for you

Functions of Noun Phrases

Just like nouns, noun phrases can be used in the following ways (as italicized).

1. As subject of a verb: *Hadiza* ate the food.
2. As direct object of a verb: They performed *an experiment*.
3. As indirect object of a verb: He gave *three of the children* some money
4. As subject complement: That exercise was *a test of the pupils' strength and endurance*.

5. As object complement: The people elected him *their leader*.
6. As complement of a preposition: Of *all the workers in the company*, he is the most dependable.
7. As an appositive to a noun or noun phrase: Diego Maradona, *the best footballer of all time*, scored the winning good.

5.2.2 Adjectival Phrases (AdjP)

An adjectival phrase is a phrase which describes a noun or a pronoun. In most cases, an adjectival phrase is a cluster of adjectives but in some other cases, we have one or more adverbs serving as an intensifier or a pre-modifier to one or more adjectives in an adjectival phrase. Still in some instances, 'An adjectival phrase is a prepositional phrase that modifies a noun or a pronoun' (Adegbija 1998, p. 135). These three possibilities are respectively exemplified by the following sentences.

    a. Daniel is an intelligent tall young boy.

    b. Lola lives in a very beautiful white duplex.

    c. Please tell the man in a black suit to come.

In example (a) above, we have a cluster of adjectives (intelligent tall young) quantifying the noun 'boy'; in (b), 'very' (an adverb) introduces the adjectival phrase qualifying the noun 'duplex' while in (c) the prepositional phrase 'in a black suit' functions as an adjectival phrase to qualify the noun 'man'.

The Structure of Adjectival Phrases

Greenbaum and Nelson (2009, p. 85) gave the following structural possibilities of adjectival phrases:

- adjective e.g. boastful, fond, long, etc.
- pre-modifier + adjective e.g. quite *boastful*
- adjective + post-modifier e.g. *boastful* of his success, *fond* of quarrlling
- pre-modifier + adjective + post-modifier e.g. too *boastful* for my liking.

From the foregoing, therefore, we may conclude that the structure of adjectival phrases is: (pre-modifier) adjective (post-modifier) which can be symbolized as (pre-m) adj (post-m).

Note that the elements in brackets are optional; only the adjective is obligatory, as in the following table.

Pre-modifier	Adjective	Post-modifier
	boastful	
quite	bad	
	fond	of quarrelling
too	boastful	for my liking

Functions of Adjectival Phrases

Broadly speaking, adjectival phrases, like adjectives, qualify/modify nouns and pronouns. However, these specific functions of adjectival phrases have been identified by Greenbaum and Nelson (2009, p. 85).

1. Pre-modifier in a noun phrase e.g. She is a *very pretty* girl.
2. Post-modifier in a noun phrase e.g. The money *available* is too little.
3. Subject complement e.g. Some of the oranges are *too rotten to eat*.

i. Object complement e.g. The news he brought made me *happy with him*.

5.2.3 Verb Phrases (VP)

A verb phrase is a phrase functioning as a verb. In Transformational Generative Grammar (TGG), the verb phrase is made up of the verb and its complement. Thus, in 'A baby is crying in the room', the verb phrase is 'is crying in the room'. On the other hand, in Systemic Functional Grammar (SFG), the verb phrase, usually called *verbal group,* is limited to the verbal elements which either consist of main/lexical verbs only or a combination of main verbs and auxiliary verbs. This latter structure of the verb phrase in SFG is what some grammarians call *verbal phrase*. In this book, we shall use terms in both TGG (verb phrase) and SFG (verbal group) interchangeably to refer to the verb phrase but its structure will be that of SFG. Note that when there is no lexical verb in a sentence, an auxiliary verb can function as a lexical verb.

a. Chinwe *cooked* the food.

b. Yusuf *has written* the note.

c. Bukola *must have been sleeping* now.

d. The people *are* happy.

In example (a) above, 'cooked' is the verb phrase but in (b) and (c), we have groups of words. While in (b) the main verb 'written' is preceded by a single auxiliary verb, in (c) the main verb 'sleeping' is preceded by three auxiliary verbs. In (d), however, the only verb is an auxiliary verb which doubles as the main verb of the sentence. We shall adopt the SFG approach in analyzing our verb phrases. This takes us to the structure of the verb phrase.

The Structure of Verb Phrases

In Systemic Grammar, the main or lexical verb is mandatory and is represented with the letter 'l' while the auxiliary verbs which are optional pre-modifiers to the lexical verb are represented with the letter 'a'. Also, the word 'not' (negator) which is used with auxiliary verbs (as in 'did not', 'is not', 'will not', 'has not', etc) is regarded as an element of the verb phrase and is thus represented with the letter 'n'. Finally, when the verb phrase has a phrasal verb, the lexical verb may be post-modified by an adverb or a preposition, usually called *particle* (pt). Thus, the structure of the verbal group in Systemic Grammar, according to Osisanwo (2002, p. 44), is: (a) (n) l (pt). It is broken down as follows.

- lexical e.g. read, plant, walk, etc.
- auxiliary + lexical e.g. has *read*, are *walking*, etc.
- auxiliary + negator + lexical .e.g. will not *go*, should not *cry*, etc.
- auxiliary + negator + lexical + particle e.g. does not *take* after, has not *given* up, etc.

The table below presents the structure of the verb phrase as discussed above.

Auxiliary	Negator	Lexical	Particle
		go	
has		read	
should	not	cry	
has	not	given	up

Greenbaum and Nelson (2009) observed that there can only be a maximum of four auxiliary verbs in a verb phrase and that they should be in this order: modal, (e.g. will), perfect (e.g. have), progressive (e.g. singing) and passive (e.g. been) as in 'She *may have been being* duped'.

Functions of Verb Phrases

According to https://www.brighthubeducation.com, the following are the major functions of verb phrases.

a. **As verb phrase head**: The head of a verb phrase is the most important word in the phrase. In the phrases following, the italicized word is the head.

   read the newspapers

   listen to me

   wise up

   to *sleep*

b. **As predicate**: A predicate is made up of at least one verb and any object, modifier and complement, as italicized in these sentences.

   The rain has stopped.

   He warned us not to tell anyone.

   Calmly, she answered all the questions.

c. **As noun phrase modifier**: Any expression that describes a noun phrase is a noun phrase modifier. Examples are in italics in the following sentences.

   Tell the lady *going upstairs* to meet me here.

   His book *written on family psychology* is a bestseller.

d. **As adjective phrase complement**: This is a verb which completes the meaning of an adjectival phrase.

Most children are happy to leave home.

Diana is eager to work with us.

I am pleased to write this letter to you.

e. **As verb phrase complement**: These complete the meaning of verb phrases, as italicized thus:

You cannot afford to lose this election.

Unscrupulous liars always lie to cover up other lies.

f. **As adverbials**: These are verb phrases providing information about time, place, reason, manner, etc on other verbs, as in the underlined sentences.

Please, shut the door to give some warmth.

To succeed in life, you have to be disciplined.

5.2.4 Adverbial Phrases (AdvP)

An adverbial phrase is a phrase used as an adverb. The most important word in an adverbial phrase is, therefore, an adverb such as 'gently' in the adverbial phrases in the sentences below:

a. Garba speaks *gently*.

b. Garba speaks *very gently*.

c. Garba speaks *very gently indeed*.

Types of Adverbial Phrases

As with adverbs, adverbial phrases can be broadly classified into adjuncts, disjuncts and conjuncts (Quirk & Greenbaum, 1973).

a. **Adjuncts**: These are integrated within or have close affinity with their sentences. They usually answer the question when, where, why, how, how often, to what extent, etc in relation to the verb of the sentence. They are thus sub-classified as:

i. **Time adjuncts** (adverbial phrases of time) answer the question 'When?' e.g. at 1 a.m., right now, in the afternoon, last year, etc.

ii. **Place adjuncts** (adverbial phrases of place) answer the question 'Where?' e.g. in China, on the roof, at home, all the way from Lagos, etc.

iii. **Reason adjuncts** (adverbial phrases of reason) answer the question 'Why?' e.g. because of him, for that reason, etc.

iv. **Intensifiers** (adverbial phrases of degree) show to what extent something happens e.g. too much, a lot, very highly, so greatly, etc.

v. **Manner adjuncts** (adverbial phrases of manner) show how something happens e.g. like this, very skilfully, in that way, indiscriminately, etc.

vi. **Frequency adjuncts** (adverbial phrases of frequency) show how often something happens e.g. quite frequently, hardly ever, twice a week, etc.

Other sub-classses of adjuncts include viewpoint adjunct, focusing adjunct, subject adjunct, etc. (See Quirk and Greenbaum, 1973, p. 210 ff.)

b. **Disjuncts:** Disjuncts are peripheral to their sentences. They usually express attitude, judgement or comments and are broadly categorized as:

i. **Style disjuncts:** Adverbial phrases or disjuncts of style include: to be frank; frankly speaking, in all honestly, seriously speaking, to put it bluntly, etc. Style disjuncts normally introduce their sentences.

ii. **Attitudinal disjuncts**: These usually convey the comment of the speaker on what he is saying e.g. of course, to my surprise, more importantly, naturally, in view of the distance, very rightly, quite certainly, fundamentally, so obviously, etc.

c. **Conjuncts:** These serve as links or connectives. Put differently, they are used as transitional markers or devices in discourse or texts for various purposes, including to: enumerate (e.g. to start with, in the second place, last but not the least), reinforce (e.g. in addition, above all), equate (e.g. in the same way, equally), sum up (e.g. in conclusion, (all) in all, in summary), show result (e.g. as a result, consequently), suggest alternatives (e.g. on the other hand, put differently), show contrast (e.g. although, in any case, in spite of that), etc.

It should be noted, as Greenbaum and Nelson (2012 p. 88) pointed out, that 'there is considerable overlap between the preposition class and the adverb class'. This is why an adverbial phrase may be introduced by a preposition or the same word may function either as an adverbial phrase or as a prepositional phrase based on the situation of use. This situation of use has been explained under the section on the multifunctionality of English words in the previous chapter.

The Structure of Adverbial Phrases

The structure of adverbial phrases is similar to that of adjectival phrases. The main or obligatory word in an adverbial phrase is an adverb. Sometimes, the adverb is pre-modified by another adverb (called 'pre-modifier') such as 'very' in 'very gently' and it may also be post-modified by another adverb (called 'post-modifier') such as 'indeed' in 'very gently indeed'. Below are the structural possibilities of adverbial phrases.

- adverb e.g. well, early, quickly, soon, etc.
- pre-modifier + adverb e.g. so *well*, quite *early*, very *quickly*, etc.
- adverb + post-modifier e.g. *slowly* indeed, *courageously* enough, etc
- pre-modifier + adverb + post-modifier e.g. so *well* indeed, quite *early* enough, very *quickly* now, etc.

The structure may, thus, be symbolized as (pre-m) adv (post-m). The table below summarizes this structure.

Pre-modifier	Adverb	Post-modifier
	quickly	
so	well	
	slowly	indeed
quite	early	enough

Functions of Adverbial Phrases

Just like adverbs, adverbial phrases can modify virtually all the parts of speech, including other adverbs. Here are some examples in italics.

1. As modifier of a verb e.g. The governor arrived *very late*. (modifying the verb 'arrived')
2. As modifier of an adjective e.g. His account of the story was *really quite* interesting. (modifying the adjective 'interesting')
3. As modifier of another adverb (phrase) e.g. She behaved *so remarkably* maturely. (modifying the adverb 'maturely')

4. As modifier of a noun (phrase) e.g. I have never seen *such a strange thing before.*

   (modifying the noun phrase 'a strange thing')

5.2.5 Prepositional Phrases (PP)

A prepositional phrase does the work of a preposition and it is headed by a preposition (where there are other words). Examples:

a. Joy is waiting *for Peace.*
b. The thieves escaped *through the window.*
c. Look *at the camera* that I bought.
d. *Of all the musicians*, Panam remains my favourite.

The Structure of Prepositional Phrases

In Transformational Generative Grammar, the prepositional phrase is made up of two obligatory elements in this order: Preposition + Noun Phrase (Prep + NP) (See Egbe, 2005 & Lamidi, 2016). The noun phrase following a preposition in a prepositional phrase is called 'complement'. It is a complement, rather than a post-modifier, because it is not optional (Greenbaum & Nelson, 2009).

It is also possible for the preposition in a prepositional phrase to be pre-modified by an adverb (phrase) such as 'right', 'straight', 'just', etc. The pre-modifier is, however, optional. The following are the various structural possibilities of prepositional phrases.

- preposition + complement e.g. *at* home, *from* London, *below* the pass mark, etc.
- pre-modifier + preposition + complement e.g. right *on* time, straight *into* the palace, very well *above* the minimum standard, etc.

Apart from the above, note also that it is possible in transformations to have 'stranded' prepositions functioning in isolation from their moved or 'fronted' complements (Greenbaum & Nelson, 2009). Examine the following sentences where the stranded prepositions are underlined and their detached complements are italicized. Try to convert them back to their active forms and note the new positions of the two elements.

The patient is being attended <u>to</u>. (passive transformation)

Where are you coming <u>from</u>. (interrogative transformation)

Here is the man *whom* I work <u>for</u>. (relative transformation)

This possibility of stranded prepositions in transformations debunks the claim of an obligatory complement in a prepositional phrase, since the preposition is usually treated independently as a prepositional phrase and its complement, independently as a noun phrase, in syntactic analysis. We may, therefore, include the stranded preposition in the structure thus:

- preposition e.g. of, from, to, at

The structure of the prepositional phrase is, therefore, (pre-modifier) preposition (complement) with the symbol: (pre-m) prep (c). This structure is summarized by the following table.

Pre-modifier	Preposition	Complement
	for	
	at	home
right	on	time

Functions of Prepositional Phrases

1. As post-modifiers of nouns e.g. The cost *of electricity* has been subsidized by the government. Teachers *at the school* are all university graduates.

2. As post-modifiers of adjectives e.g. I am aware *of all his gimmicks*. He was very much pleased *with his son's results*.

3. As adverbials e.g. *In my opinion*, the salary is too little. She works *from sunrise to sunset*.

Other less common types of phrase are next. They are not recognized by TGG and SFG but they have been identified by some other grammarians and you should be familiar with them. As a matter of fact, we can say that they are offshoots of the types of phrase already discussed.

5.2.6 Appositive Phrases (AP)

An appositive phrase is a kind of noun phrase that is used in reference to a noun (phrase). It usually follows the noun (phrase) which it refers to or gives information on. Also, it is normally separated from the rest of the sentence with commas or brackets.

a. Awolowo, the first Premier of Western Nigeria, was a nationalist.

b. Chimamanda Adichie, a talented novelist, won the prize.

c. Jim Ovia founded Zenith Bank, one of the best banks in the country.

In (a) above, 'the first Premier of Western Nigeria' is appositive to 'Awolowo', in (b) 'a talented novelist' is in apposition to 'Chimamanda Adichie' while in (c), 'one of the best banks in the country' is appositive to 'Zenith Bank'. Note, also, that appositive phrases can be removed from the rest of their sentences without affecting the meaning of the sentences, thus:

Awolowo was a nationalist.

Chimamanda Adichie won the prize.

Jim Ovia founded Zenith Bank.

The Structure of Appositive Phrases

Since appositive phrases are a kind of noun phrases, they have exactly the same structural pattern of (m) h (q) as noun phrases. Examples:

- headword e.g. premier, she, crocodiles
- modifier + headword e.g. the *crocodiles*, a talented *novelist*
- headword + qualifier e.g. *people* from all walks of life
- modifier + headword + qualifier e.g. one of the best *banks* in the country

The table following summarizes this.

Modifier	Headword	Qualifier
	premier	
a talented	novelist	
	people	from all walks of life
one of the best	banks	in the country

5.2.7 Gerundial Phrases (GP)

In the words of Adegbija (1998, p. 119), 'A gerund phrase is made up of a gerund and its complement and any modifiers'. This implies that the head of this phrase is a gerund which is the obligatory part of the phrase. Besides, the word 'complement' here implies a post-modifier while 'modifier' means 'pre-modifier'. Therefore, a gerund(ial) phrase is a kind of noun phrase which consists of a gerund, as well as an optional (pre)modifier and/or complement.

a. Niyi enjoys *playing table tennis* on a hot afternoon.
b. *The counting of voters* is done by electoral officers.

The gerund phrase in (a) above is made up of the gerund 'playing' and its complement 'table tennis' while that in (b) is made up of the gerund 'counting' its (pre) modifier 'the' and its complement 'of voters'.

The Structure of Gerundial Phrases

As explained above, a gerundial phrase is headed by a gerund and has on optional post-modifier/complement and an optional (pre) modifier. These can be structurally represented as (m) g (c). The structure is broken down as follows:

- gerund e.g. running, cooking
- gerund + complement e.g. *playing* table tennis, *cooking* beans
- modifier + gerund e.g. the *counting*, his *spelling*
- modifier + gerund + complement e.g. the *counting* of voters, your *sleeping* outside

Modifier	Gerund	Complement
	running	
	playing	table tennis
the	counting	
the	counting	of voters

5.2.8 Infinitival Phrases (IP)

As earlier explained, an infinitive may comprise the word 'to' and a main verb e.g. to read, to eat, to dance, to live, to see, etc. The infinitive is a form of the verb and it is so called because it is not limited to a particular person or tense (Fakuade, 2012, p. 202). The infinitive phrase, then, may be defined as a form of verb phrase that consists of an infinitive, with or without a modifier and/or complement as in:

a. *To pass the exam* you must work hard.

b. Joshua is always ready *to help*.

The Structure of Infinitival Phrases

The structure of infinitival phrases may be represented with the symbol: (m) i (c). This means an optional modifier, an obligatory infinitive and an optional complement, as in:

- infinitive e.g. to come, to share
- modifier + infinitive e.g. just *to eat*, so as *to help*
- infinitive + complement e.g. *to pass* the exam, *to help* them
- modifier + infinitive + complement e.g. in order *to pass* the exam, just *to eat* our food

This is as presented in the table below.

Modifier	Infinitive	Complement
	to help	
so as	to help	
	to pass	the exam
in order	to pass	the exam

5.2.9 Participial Phrases (ParP)

A participle is a word that "'participates' in the characteristics of both verb and adjective" (Crystal, 2015, p. 352). Participles are verbs in their 'ing' or 'en' form, used as adjectives and are normally referred to as *verbal adjectives*. Similarly, therefore, a participial phrase is a kind of adjectival phrase which has a participle and any complement or modifier. Participial phrases can be categorized into two: those in 'ing' form are present participial phrases while those in 'en' form are past participial phrases.

Present Participial Phrases

   i. *Dancing round the hall*, the senator shook hands with everybody.
   ii. The winner, *looking at the cheering huge crowd*, shed tears of joy.

Past Participial Phrases

   iii. *Beaten by the teacher*, Helen cried profusely.
   iv. Francis threw a party, *overwhelmed by the news of his success*.

The Structure of Participial Phrases

For the structure of participial phrases, the following symbol may be used: (m) par (c). Remember that either a verb in its 'ing' form or one in its 'en' form (a participle) is the head of a participial phrase. The verb may then be preceded by a modifier or followed by a complement which is usually a noun phrase or a prepositional phrase, as broken down below.

- participle e.g. overwhelmed, dancing
- participle + complement e.g. *depressed* by his loss, *dancing* round the hall
- modifier + participle e.g. having *danced*, having *gone*

- modifier + participle + complement e.g. having *taken* the drug, having *danced* round

The following table shows the structure of participial phrases.

Modifier	Participle	Complement
	overwhelmed	
	dancing	round the hall
having	danced	
having	taken	the drug

Participial phrases are a good way of varying the structure of our sentences and of ensuring economy of words. Participles, gerunds and infinitives are called *verbals* because they are 'forms of verbs that are used as other parts of speech' (Strumpf & Douglas (n.d.), p. 151). A good way of differentiating between ordinary verbs in their 'ing' or 'en' form and participles in the same form is that the verbs are usually preceded by a helping verb but the participles are not (Fakuade, 2012, p. 201). Compare the italicized non-participial structures in the sentences below with those in (i) and (iii) above:

The senator was *dancing round the hall*.

Helen has been *beaten by the teacher*.

5.2.10 Determiner Phrases (DP): A Proposition

Determiners have already been discussed in chapter three. The pre-occupation of this section is to propose determiners as a type of phrases in English. Unlike in some theories of Generative Grammar where 'determiner is regarded as the head in combination with a noun, to produce a determiner phrase (DP)' and where noun phrases are seen as 'projections of the determiner'

(Crystal, 2015, p. 140), our pre-occupation here is to present groups of determiners without a noun as phrases in their own right. The following reasons are advanced for this proposition.

1. The determiner has been established as a separate word class in English just like nouns, adjectives, verbs, adverbs and prepositions. Like these parts of speech, all of which expand to form phrases, the determiner is also capable of expanding to be a phrase as in: the first two, the last few, twice an, his last three, all the four, etc.

2. In the modern sense, just like the other phrases (noun phrases, adverbial phrases adjectival phrases, etc) determiner phrases may either be made up of single words (such as: a, the, my, her, all, both, some, much, two, ten, first, third, etc) or groups of words (e.g. all the, both my, the six, those ten, your two, all our, half a, the many, those few, two little, all the four, the first two, those last twenty, all the other, etc.

3. A phrase is normally defined as a group of words without a (finite) verb. Besides, it does not make full meaning and forms part of a sentence. Groups of determiners (determiner phrases), such as those italicized in the following sentences, have no verb, neither do they make full sense on their own and they form part of their sentences.

Give me *the first two* biros.

He was *twice an* HOD in the college.

The last few minutes of the exam was filled with tension.

His first three examples were very apt.

The government has paid *all the one hundred and fifty* sacked workers.

4. Just like many of the other phrases, the determiner phrase is a multi-headed phrase. For instance, in the adjectival phrase 'intelligent tall fair Nigerian' (lady) each of the adjectives can independently function as the head of the phrase to qualify the noun 'lady' thus: intelligent (lady), tall (lady), fair (lady), Nigerian (lady). In the same vein, any of the determiners in a determiner phrase can be the head of the phrase e.g. in 'all the five little' (babies), any of the determiners can be used with 'babies' as head of the phrase thus: all (babies), the (babies), five (babies), little (babies).
5. In terms of size, among the word classes in the closed class, the class of determiners is the largest, with over ten sub-classes.

It is important to state that even though we have tried to analyze the structure of each phrase separately with a different nomenclature, it is possible to use the following pattern for the structure of any English phrase: (Premodifier) Head (Postmodifier).

Phrase	Premodifier	Head	Postmodifier
Noun phrase	the	person	with a red cap
Adjectival phrase	very	beautiful	indeed
Adverbial phrase	so	wisely	enough
Verb phrase	has	come	across
Prepositional phrase	straight	into	the palace
Gerundial Phrase	the	counting	of voters
Appositive Phrase	a Nigerian	novelist	in the UK
Infinitival Phrase	in order	to pass	the exam

Participial Phrase	having been	beaten	by the teacher

Note, as earlier explained, that only the head of a phrase is obligatory; the others are optional.

Revision Exercise 13

1. What is a phrase?
   a. Argue for or against the notion that while every word may be a phrase, not every phrase is a word.
2. Define the following types of phrase and give two examples of each: (a) Adjectival Phrase (b) Prepositional Phrase (c) Adverbial Phrase (d) Appositive Phrase (e) Determiner Phrase
3. Identify the structures of these phrases and give one example of each: (a) Noun Phrase (b) Verb Phrase (c) Prepositional Phrase (d) Adverbial Phrase (e) Infinitival Phrase
4. With four points and convincing examples, justify the proposition for determiner phrase.
5. From the passage below, identify two examples of each of the following types of phrase and state their functions: (a) Noun Phrase (b) Adverbial Phrase (c) Prepositional Phrase (d) Gerundial Phrase (e) Participial Phrase

After Ugwu watched Master drive out of the compound, he went and stood beside the radiogram and looked at it carefully, without touching it. Then he walked around the house, up and down, touching books and curtains and furniture and plates, and when it got dark, he turned the light on and marvelled at how bright the bulb that dangled from the ceiling was, how it did not cast long shadows on the wall like the palm oil lamps back home. His mother would be preparing the evening meal now, pounding *akpu* in the mortar, the pestle grasped tightly with both hands. Chioke, the junior wife, would be tending the pot of watery soup balanced on three stones over the fire. The children would have come back from the stream and would be taunting and chasing one another under the breadfruit tree. Perhaps Amulika would be watching them. She was the oldest child in the household now, and as they all sat around the fire to eat, she would break up the fights when the younger ones struggled over the strips of dried fish in the soup. She would wait until all the *akpu* was eaten. And then divide the fish so that each child had a piece, and she would keep the biggest for herself, as he had always done.

(An excerpt from *Half of a Yellow Sun* by Chimamanda Ngozi Adichie, 2006, p. 7)

Chapter Six

THE CLAUSE

6.1 The Meaning of Clause

Just like the phrase, Traditional Grammar conceives of a clause as a group of words, but this is not so in modern linguistics. For example, Systemic Grammar views a clause as an expression which consists of a predicator/verb with or without other elements, and which forms a sentence or part of a sentence. This means that only the predicator, which may be a single word, is mandatory in a major clause (Osisanwo, 2002, p. 30). The clause comes immediately after the phrase up the grammatical rankscale and every clause contains at least one phrase. This leads us to a discussion of the structure of the clause. Note that the clause is not a prominent feature in TGG but it is in SFG.

6.2 The Structure of the Clause

Every clause in Systemic Functional Grammar has the structure (Subject), Predicator, (Complement) and (Adjunct), usually abbreviated as (S) P (C) (A). Note that the elements in brackets are optional. Note also that the arrangement is not fixed, as it is possible to have any of P, PC, SP, SPC, PCA, ASPC, SPCA, etc as the structure of a clause. Consider, for example:

    a. Read (P)
    b. Kayode S) read (P)

c. Kayode (S) read (P) the book (C)

d. Kayode (S) read (P) the book (C) silently (A)

e. Because (A) he (S) was (P) in the library (C)

In modern grammar, it is possible for a single word to function as a (free) morpheme, word, phrase/group, clause or even sentence. This is why, according to Halliday and Matthiessen (2014, p. 9), '*Come!* is a clause consisting of one group consisting of one word consisting of one morpheme.' Similarly, therefore, all the above expressions from (a) to (e) are clauses. In (a), we have only the predicator 'Read' but (b) to (e) have other elements apart from their predicators. Note that while Adjunct comes last in (d), it comes first in (e). This is because of the mobility associated with adjuncts, as earlier discussed. The following explains the elements of the structure of the clause.

Subject: This is made up of nouns, noun phrases and pronouns as doers of actions.

Predicator: This is made up of verbs and verb phrases.

Complement: This slot is occupied by nouns, noun phrases, pronouns and adjectives, used as object or complement of the sentence.

Adjunct: This consists of adverbs, adverbial phrases, prepositions and prepositional phrases.

As you might have observed, the clauses in (a) to (d) above convey full meaning and can stand on their own while the one in (e) cannot. For (e) to make complete sense, another clause has to be added to it thus:

a. Kayode read the book silently (1) because he was in the library (2).

These two different types of clause will be the focus of our next sub-topic.

6.3 Types of Clause

6.3.1 Independent Clause

This is a clause that makes complete thought and can stand on its own. Some linguists consider this type of clause as a 'simple kernel sentence' (Babatunde, 2003, p. 107) and it is the reason why a clause may be a sentence. The independent clause is also known as main/superordinate/principal/alpha clause and it is represented with the alpha symbol

(∂) in SFG. Examples (a) to (d) above are independent clauses.

6.3.2 Dependent Clause

This is a clause that does not make complete sense and can, therefore, not stand on its own such as the clause in (e) above. Other examples are:

when it rains

before it is too late

if you don't come

what he knows

A dependent clause needs an independent clause to convey full meaning, as in (f) above. The dependent clause is also called subordinate/beta clause and is represented with the beta symbol (β) in SFG. It is of the following sub-types.

    A. **Nominal Dependent Clauses:** Also simply known as 'nominal clauses' or 'noun clauses', these are clauses used as nouns. Note the following qualities of noun clauses:

- They are usually introduced by relative pronouns such as: who, why, when, how, that, etc.
- They can usually be replaced by the pronoun 'it' or some modification of it.
- They usually answer the question 'What?'

The italicized expressions in these sentences are noun clauses.

1. He knows where she hid the gold ring.
2. What he did was very wrong.
3. That he still lies after so much torture baffles me.
4. We want to know how you did it.
5. I know who your girlfriend is.

Let us see if the clauses above have the three attributes of noun clauses earlier on enumerated. We shall only do this with the first example. Do the same thing with the other ones.

- Noun clauses are usually introduced by relative pronouns. 'Where' (a relative pronoun) introduces this.
- They can usually be replaced by 'it'. If we replace the clause with 'it', what we have is 'He knows *it*'.
- They usually answer the question 'What?' To do this, replace the noun clause with the question word 'what' and convert the sentence to a declarative question. The answer to the question will be the replaced noun clause e.g.

    Question: He knows *wha*t?

    Answer: Where she hid the ring.

Note that the three qualities of noun clauses relate to pronouns and this further demonstrates the relationship between nouns and pronouns.

Types of Noun Clause

Noun clauses can be classified based on the kind of word(s) that introduce(s) them. The following are the types of noun clause, according to Quirk and Greenbaum (1973, p. 316 ff.)

    a. **That-clauses** are introduced by the pronoun 'that' e.g. Nobody believed *that Seth Rollins could beat Brock Lesnar.*

    b. **Wh-interrogative clauses** are introduced by wh-question words e.g. *Why he did it* is everybody's concern.

    c. **Yes-no interrogative clauses** are introduced by 'if' or 'whether' e.g. Do you know *if/whether it will rain today?*

    d. **Nominal relative clauses** usually start with wh-elements e.g. Ask me for *whatever you need.*

    e. **Nominal-ing clauses** are participial clauses starting with an ing-verb e.g. She likes *making new friends* wherever she goes.

    f. **To-infinitive nominal clauses** are infinitival clauses introduced by 'to' e.g. His new job – *to clean the house and wash the clothes* – is demeaning.

Functions of Noun Clauses

Noun clauses perform the same functions as nouns and noun phrases, principally as subject, object or complement in their sentences.

    i. Noun clause as subject of a verb e.g. *What he did* was very wrong.

ii. Noun clause as object of a verb e.g. Isaiah disclosed *whom he would marry*.
iii. Noun clause as object of a preposition e.g. I am happy for *what God has done for me*.
iv. Noun clause as complement of a verb e.g. That's *how to behave in public*.
v. Noun clause in apposition to a noun (phrase) e.g. His new job – *to clean the house and wash the clothes* – is demeaning.

B. **Adjectival Dependent Clauses**: They are clauses that function as adjectives. Such clauses are also called 'adjectival clauses' or 'relative clauses'. These attributes will help you in identifying adjectival dependent clauses.

- They usually start with relative pronouns such as: who, whose, whom, which, that, etc. This is why they are also known as relative clauses.
- If removed, they do not affect the meaning of their sentences.
- They qualify a noun or pronoun in their sentences

Below are examples of adjectival clauses in italics.

1. Do you know the man *that drove this car here*?
2. One of the houses *which Ayanfe built* is a duplex.
3. The doctor, *who discovered the cure for the pandemic*, is a Nigerian.
4. Mr Venn, *whose house we lodged in*, works at the academy.

Let us now see if the relative clauses will meet the criteria already stated for relative clauses. We shall try this with example (1) above.

> Adjectival clauses usually start with relative pronouns: The relative pronoun 'that' starts the clause.

> If removed, adjectival clauses do not affect the meaning of their sentences: Do you know the man?

> They qualify a noun or pronoun: In (1) above, the adjectival clause qualifies the noun 'man'.

Types of Adjectival Clauses

On the types of adjectival clauses, Quirk and Greenbaum (1973) have this to say:

> Modification can be restrictive or non-restrictive. That is, the head can be viewed as a member of a class which can be linguistically identified only through the modification that has been supplied (*restrictive*). Or the head can be viewed as unique or as a member of a class that has been independently identified (for example in a preceding sentence); any modification given to such a head is additional information which is not essential for identifying the head, and we call it *non-restrictive* (p. 376).

From the excerpt above, two kinds of adjectival clauses can be differentiated: restrictive and non-restrictive adjectival clauses. These are discussed next.

1. **Restrictive Adjectival Clauses** are those whose heads or antecedents depend on such clauses for interpretation and they can, therefore, not be separated from their heads to derive full meaning. For example, to identify the man

mentioned in (1) above, we need to know that he 'drove this car here'. The restrictive adjectival clause is also called 'defining adjectival clause'. Examples (1) and (2) above are restrictive adjectival clauses.

2. **Non-Restrictive Adjectival Clauses** are those whose heads can be identified without reference to the clauses. In other words, the heads of such clauses are independent of their modifiers which only give additional information to the reader or hearer. To identify the doctor in example (3) above, the clause 'who discovered the cure for the pandemic' is not necessary perhaps because somewhere before now, allusion has been made to his discovery which the speaker is only emphasizing here. Non-restrictive adjectival clauses, also known as 'non-defining adjectival clauses', are usually separated from their main clauses with commas, dashes or parentheses in writing or with tone units in speech. Examples (3) and (4) above are non-restrictive adjectival clauses.

Functions of Adjectival Clauses

Like adjectives and adjectival phrases, adjectival clauses qualify/modify their antecedent nouns and pronouns. For instance, in the sentence 'The lady *whose bag was snatched* is a journalist', the adjectival clause in italics qualifies the noun 'lady'. Likewise, in the sentence 'He *who must come to equity* must come with clean hands', the italicized adjectival clause modifies the pronoun 'he' in the sentence.

C. **Adverbial Dependent Clauses:** An adverbial dependent clause is a clause used as an adverb and it is also known as 'adverbial clause'. Like the adverb and the adverbial phrase, the adverbial clause can be broadly classified into three: adjuncts, disjuncts and conjuncts.

a. **Adjuncts** is the commonest group of adverbials used to show time, place, reason, manner, degree, etc and they are, therefore, named accordingly.

   i. **Time adjuncts** or adverbial clauses of time show when an action or event takes place e.g. I saw Bola *when she sneaked in. Before you eat*, wash your hands.

   ii. **Place adjuncts** or adverbial clauses of place show where an action happens e.g. Put the key *where you can easily see it. Wherever you go* I will go.

   iii. Adverbial clauses of place can be replaced by 'there' e.g. Put the key *there. There* I will go.

   iv. **Reason adjuncts** or adverbial clauses of reason indicate why something happens e.g. The man was hanged *because he committed murder. Since your mother is not at home*, you are to cook the meals.

   v. **Manner adjuncts** or adverbial clauses of manner show how an action happens e.g. You may do *as you wish*. She fidgets *like a robber that has been caught red handed*.

   vi. **Frequency adjuncts** or adverbial clauses of frequency disclose how often something takes place e.g. She travels to Dubai *as often as she likes. As regularly as it is possible*, go for a medical check-up.

   vii. **Condition adjuncts** or adverbial clauses of condition give a condition for doing something. They are usually introduced by if, whether or unless e.g. Come with me *if you want to. Unless they finish the job*, they will not be paid.

viii. **Concession adjuncts** or adverbial clauses of concession show that something is true or will be allowed even if a particular condition has not been met. They are usually introduced by words like (al)though, even though, despite, etc. e.g. *Although he is poor*, he is happy. *Despite that it was raining heavily*, he managed to go to school.

b. **Disjuncts** is the second class of adverbial clauses. Unlike adjuncts, disjuncts are peripheral to the structure of their sentences and usually assess or evaluate the form or content of communication. They are of two types: style disjuncts and attitudinal disjuncts.

   i. **Style disjuncts**, according to Quirk and Greenbaum (1973, p. 242), 'convey the speaker's comment on the form of what he is saying, defining in some way under what conditions he is talking'. Examples of style disjuncts include: *If I may say so*, you don't deserve that woman. *If I can speak generally*, the election was free and fair.

   ii. **Attitudinal disjuncts** comment on the content of communication. Based on this, it may be said that the difference between style disjuncts and attitudinal disjuncts lies in form and content respectively. Examples of attitudinal disjuncts are italicized in these sentences. *What is more fascinating*, the candidate holds a PhD degree from Harvard University. General elections might not hold next year *with the crises that are happening in various parts of the country*.

c. **Conjuncts** serve various connective or linking purposes in texts which include:

i. **Enumerative** e.g. *The first step to success in life is* ensure that you are diligent.

ii. **Reinforcing** e.g. *Above all that I have said*, be disciplined.

iii. **Result** e.g. *Consequent upon what happened,* he resigned.

iv. **Apposition** e.g. *That is (to say)*, we are already late.

Other kinds of conjunct, according to Quirk and Greenbaum (1973, pp. 247-248), are: equative, transitional, summative, inferential, reformulatory, replacive, antithetic, concessive and temporal transition.

Note: Even though Quirk and Greenbaum (1973) classified adverbials into adjuncts, disjuncts and conjuncts, they did not differentiate adverbials used as single words from those used as phrases or clauses. Therefore, we would like to propose the following:

- **Lexical adjuncts/disjuncts/conjuncts** for adverbials used as single, individual words (adverbs).
- **Phrasal adjuncts/disjuncts/conjuncts** for adverbials functioning as phrases (adverbial phrases).
- **Clausal adjuncts/disjuncts/conjuncts** for adverbials functioning as clauses (adverbial clauses).

Functions of Adverbial Clauses

Like adverbs and adverbial phrases, adverbial clauses modify/qualify verbs, adjectives, nouns, other adverbs, etc.

1. Adverbial Clauses Modifying Verbs

Doyin will go *anywhere you send her*. (Adverbial clause of place modifying the verb 'go').

He fidgets *like a robber that has been caught red-handed.* (Adverbial clause of manner modifying the verb 'fidgets')

2. **Adverbial Clauses Modifying Adjectives**

   Although they are children, they are mature. (Adverbial clause of concession modifying the adjective 'mature')

   Above all that I have said, be disciplined. (Adverbial clause of reinforcement qualifying the adjective 'disciplined')

3. **Adverbial Clauses Modifying Adverbs**

   If you switch off the lights, then, I will go out. (Adverbial clause of condition modifying the adverb 'then')

   Jemimah behaves more courteously *than all the girls that came.* (Adverbial clause of comparison qualifying the adverb 'courteously')

D. Verbless Dependent Clauses: These are also simply referred to as 'verbless clauses'. A verbless clause is one with an ellipted form of the verb 'be' and sometimes, also an omitted subject which is usually recoverable or inferable from the context or sentence (Quirk and Greenbaum, 1973). It may be said, therefore, that a verbless clause is a clause with an implicit or invisible verb and/or subject. Verbless clauses are regarded as clauses 'because they can be analyzed in terms of one or more clause elements' (Leech & Svartvik, 2012, p. 262). The italicized expressions in the following sentences are verbless clauses. Their full forms are enclosed in brackets opposite them.

Whether cold or hot, serve the food. (Whether it is cold or not ...)

When in London, I met Halliday. (When I was in London ...)

This man sounds convincing *even if lying*. (... even if he is lying).

Terrified, the glass fell off his hand. (Because he was terrified ...)

The phenomenon involved in most verbless clauses, as those above, is technically known as 'dangling modifier'. This is a situation whereby there is a modifier in a structure but its head or subject of the verb is absent, thus leaving the modifier 'stranded' or 'dangling'.

Revision Exercise 14

1. Distinguish between independent clause and dependent clause and cite examples of each.
2. Elaborately discuss the structure of the clause and cite relevant examples.
3. Explain any four types of dependent clause and give two instances of each.
4. Identify from the passage below, two instances of each of these types of clause and give their functions as used in the host sentences: (a) Noun Clause (b) Adjectival Clause (c) Adverbial Clause

Of course, when we speak of this shift, this positive advance in political consciousness, which is very discriminating in its identification of national enemies, we have to continue to caution against the increasingly desperate activities of that handful of political leadership who are determined that the retrogressive status be maintained. Their tactics vary from crude tribal demagoguery to economic red herrings. They do not hesitate, for instance, to explain away the widespread poverty in the nation as selective deprivation which is limited to their section of the country only and thus a direct consequence of the monopoly of national resources by yet another section of the nation. In 1982, a brief respite was brought by an external shift in their sectionalizing through the inhuman expulsion of millions of aliens, Ghanaians being the worst sufferers in the unprecedented exodus. The last of such scapegoats having departed, there had to be recourse to internal villainy for the consolidation of the geographical bases these politicians represent. That they have failed so far was decidedly proved when the people were robbed of their hopes for a change of government in the most cynical non-election in the brief history of national existence.

(Adapted from *The Man Died* by Wole Soyinka, 1985, p. xx)

Chapter Seven

THE SENTENCE

7.1 Sentence Defined

Sentence corresponds to 'clause complex' in Systemic Functional Grammar (Butt, Fahey, Spinks & Yallop 1995). The sentence is one of the most difficult concepts to define in linguistics. Confirming this, Fries (1952) cited in Tomori (1977, p. 19), observed that 'more than two hundred different definitions of sentence confront the worker who undertakes to deal with the structure of English utterance'. There are notional, phonological, orthographic, semantic, contextual, grammatical, physiological and other dimensions to the description of English sentences. However, Bloomfield's definition, as cited in Tomori (1977, p. 20), which is based on grammatical independence, has enjoyed widespread popularity among many linguists. According to Bloomfield (1933), 'Each sentence is an independent linguistic form, not included by virtue of any grammatical construction in any larger linguistic form'. In contrast to the word, therefore, the sentence is the 'maximal free form' (Crystal, 2015, p. 522). This is because the sentence is the largest unit on the grammatical rankscale. A sentence comprises one or more clauses.

An 'independent linguistic form' should be meaningful and, of course, should have a beginning and an end. Therefore, in line with Bloomfield's definition, and for our own purpose in this book, we shall attempt a semantico-orthographic definition of the sentence as a meaningful expression that starts with a capital letter and ends with a full stop, question mark or exclamation mark. Each of the following expressions, therefore, qualifies as a sentence:

    a. God is good.

    b. How old are you?

    c. Run!

The symbol for the sentence in TGG is (S) while that of SFG is the Greek sigma (Σ).

7.2 The Structure of the Sentence

Every sentence is made up of one or more clauses. Where there is one, the one clause is an independent clause (IC) and where there are more clauses, the others are either independent or dependent clauses (DC), as exemplified below:

The man committed a crime (IC).

The man committed a crime (IC) and (he) hired a lawyer (IC).

The man hired a lawyer (IC) because he committed a crime (DC).

The man committed a crime (IC) and (he) hired a lawyer (IC) who would defend him in court (DC).

7.3 Classification of Sentences

There are two popular criteria for classifying sentences: function and structure. We are proposing the third criterion of size. These three will be discussed in turn.

7.3.1 Classification of Sentences Based on Function

1. **Declarative Sentences:** These are also called 'statements'. They are expressions that may either be true or false and they normally end with a full stop. Examples of declaratives are: Your food tastes good. Her scarf was made from cotton. A medical doctor is a saviour.
2. **Interrogative Sentences:** Also called 'questions', sentences of this kind require an answer. Interrogative sentences normally end with question marks. Questions are of different kinds such as: Yes-No or Polar Questions e.g. Do you speak Chinese?; Wh-Questions e.g. What is this?; Declarative Questions e.g. Today is Monday?; Tag Questions as italicized in the sentence 'You are ill, *aren't you*?'
3. **Exclamative Sentences:** These express strong feelings such as love, hatred, anger, surprise, etc. Most exclamations start with 'what' or 'how' and end with an exclamation mark e.g. How time flies! What a brilliant performance! Wow! Alas!
4. **Imperative Sentences:** Imperatives correspond to commands and requests. Imperative commands may end with a full stop, question mark or exclamation mark (depending on the speaker's/writer's emotion) but imperative requests usually end with a full stop or a question mark as follows:

Commands: Stop! Open the gate. Will you stop the noise?

Requests: Please, be punctual. May I come in?

7.3.2 Classification of Sentences Based on Structure

1. **Simple Sentence:** This kind of sentence is made up of a single independent or main clause which expresses a single idea e.g.
   a. Ronke went to the market (IC). She bought some foodstuffs (IC).
   b. Mike had a car crash (IC). He was not hurt (IC).
2. **Compound Sentence:** A compound sentence consists of two or more independent or main clauses that convey two or more ideas. It is usually two or more simple sentences joined together by a coordinating conjunction such as: and, but, or, yet, etc as in:
   a. Ronke went to the market (IC) and (she) bought some foodstuffs (IC).
   b. Mike had a car crash (IC) but (he) was not hurt (IC).
3. **Complex Sentence:** This comprises one main or independent clause and one or more subordinate or dependent clauses, expressing two or more ideas. The subordinate clauses in a complex sentence are usually introduced by subordinating conjunctions like who, when, that, because, which, if, although, why, before, etc. Examples are:
   a. When Ronke went to the market (DP), she bought some foodstuffs (IC).
   b. Mike had a car crash (IC) although he was not hurt (DC).
4. **Compound-Complex Sentence:** This is a sentence that contains at least two independent clauses and at least one dependent clause e.g.

a. When Ronke went to the market (DP), she bought some foodstuffs (IC) and (she) cooked a sumptuous meal (IC).

b. Mike had a car crash (IC) but he was not hurt (IC) because he was on a seat belt (DP).

Note: Some authors have also identified 'multiple sentence' and 'multiple-complex sentence' (See Osisanwo, 2002 & https://akademia.com.ng/types-sentences-according-structure-examples, 2017) but their definitions of the sentence types and examples given only correspond with those of compound sentences (for multiple sentences) and compound-complex sentences (for multiple-complex sentences). For instance, Osisanwo (2002, p. 23) defined a multiple sentence as one that 'has three or more coordinated thoughts expressed in three or more independent clauses' and one of the examples he gave is 'Bala cut the grass, raked the garden and swept the house'. Remember that our definition of compound sentence, like his, allows it to have two or more independent clauses. More than two independent clauses presupposes three or more and the example given, therefore, is a compound sentence with three independent clauses.

Similarly, https://akademia.com.ng/types-sentences-according-structure-examples, (2017) submitted that 'A multiple-complex sentence has three main, independent or alpha clauses plus at least one subordinate, dependent or beta clause'. Again, this definition is a repetition of that of a compound-complex sentence which is capable of having at least two independent clauses (hence two, three or even more independent clauses) and at least one dependent clause. Therefore, its example 'If the lawyers had not moved fast, the innocent man would have been ridiculed, made to refund the money he did not steal and thrown into prison' is a compound-complex sentence.

Finally, on this section, note that the length of a sentence does not determine its type. A simple sentence may be long and a compound-complex sentence may be short thus:

    a. Doctor Goodluck Jonathan, a former President and Commander-in-Chief of the Armed Forces of the Federal Republic of Nigeria, honourably conceded defeat to General Muhammadu Buhari in the 2015 presidential election. (Simple sentence)

    b. I came, saw and conquered because God helped me. (Compound-complex sentence)

Note that while writing, your ability to use sentences of various types and lengths adds colour to your writing. You are, therefore, encouraged to vary your sentence types and lengths skilfully in writing.

7.3.3 Classification of Sentences Based on Size

Apart from the above conventional classifications of sentences, we would like to propose major and minor sentence types on the basis of size. Osisanwo (2002) has identified minor sentences but the presence of minor sentences presupposes 'major sentences'. These two are treated in this typology.

    A. **Major Sentences:** All sentences under the other two categories of English sentences (classifications of sentences according to function and structure) are major sentences. In other words, all declarative, interrogative, exclamatory, imperative, simple, compound, complex and compound-complex sentences are major sentences.

    B. **Minor Sentences:** These are mostly single words or groups of words which do not have the traditional properties of a sentence such as a subject and a predicate but which also make sense in their context of use and are independent in their own right. They also include dependent clauses used as sentences. Osisanwo (2002, pp. 23-24) identified three types of minor sentences but only the following two are applicable to our discussion here.

    i. **Completive Minor Sentences**: These sentences have been called 'fragmentary sentences' by Greenbaum and Nelson (2009, p. 207). Note, however, that fragmentary sentences are different from 'sentence fragments', a type of syntactic errors discussed in Chapter Nine. Completive minor sentences, such as those by 'Child' below, are normally used as responses in conversations.

Parent: Who is your new teacher?

Child: Mr Philip.

Parent: When did he join the school?

Child: Last week.

Parent: Do you like him?

Child: No.

Parent: Why?

Child: Because he beats me.

    ii. **Aphoristic Minor Sentences**: Here, we have truisms such as aphorisms, axioms, maxims, and the like which are short, sharp phrases used as sentences. Examples are: The more, the merrier. Better late than never. The earlier, the better. Early to bed, early to rise. Once beaten, twice shy.

7.4 The Structure of Simple Sentences

A basic simple sentence is technically called *kernel sentence*. According to Chomsky's Transformational Generative Grammar, it is a sentence that has not undergone any form of transformation such as transformation into questions, passivization, relativization, etc through the processes of insertion, deletion, substitution, etc (Lamidi, 2016 & Egbe, 2005). Aremo (2010) gave the following nine patterns of basic simple sentences in English. We should note that the patterns are a blend of Structural Grammar's Subject Verb Object Adjunct (SVOA) and Systemic Functional Grammar's Subject Predicate Complement Adjunct (SPCA). However, unlike Halliday's flexible SPCA structure of the clause, Aremo's pattern of a simple sentence is relatively fixed. This means its parts are arranged in a definite order that cannot be altered.

Pattern 1

Subject	Predicator
Wilson	came.

Pattern 2

Subject	Predicator	Direct Object
A girl	fetched	the water.

Pattern 3

Subject	Predicator	Indirect Object	Direct Object
They	elected	Pius	their new king.

Pattern 4

Subject	Predicator	Subject Complement

		[Nominal]
That fellow	is	a traitor.

Pattern 5

Subject	Predicator	Subject Complement [Adjectival]
We	are	tired.

Pattern 6

Subject	Predicator	Adverbial
Mr Okoro	lies	at will.

Pattern 7

Subject	Predicator	Direct Object	Object Complement [Nominal]
Many	consider	the teacher	a kind person.

Pattern 8

Subject	Predicator	Direct Object	Object Complement [Adjectival]
I	found	your advice	very helpful.

Pattern 9

Subject	Predicator	Direct Object	Adverbial
The man	would have given	my books	to her.

The above sentence patterns can be summarized using the formula or mnemonic below:

$$S \ P \ O_i^d \ C_{o2}^{s2} \ A_2$$

The S in the mnemonic above stands for Subject while the P stands for Predicate. These two are common to all the patterns 1 to 9. There are two types of Object, represented by the letter O with a superscript and a subscript. The superscript (^{d}) means Direct Object while the subscript ($_i$) means Indirect Object. Direct Object features in patterns 2, 3, 7, 8 and 9 but indirect object only features in pattern 3. Also, two types of Complement, represented by C, with the superscript (^{s2}) and the subscript ($_{o2}$) are obtainable; the two types are Subject Complement (C^s) and Object Complement (C_o). The number (2) co-occurring with the superscript and subscript means there are two of each type - one nominal subject complement and one adjectival subject complement and then, one nominal object complement and one adjectival object complement. We have complements in patterns 4, 5, 7 and 8. Finally, letter A for Adjunct has a subscript ($_2$) which stands for two adverbials, as we have in patterns 6 and 9.

7.5 Tree Diagrams in Syntax

One of the most prominent methods of analysis in syntax, which is especially common among transformational and systemic grammarians, is the use of tree diagrams. Tree diagrams are a systematic way of showing the structural constituents of phrases, clauses and, especially, sentences in a hierarchical order. In tree diagrams, the syntactic categories of phrase, clause and sentence are presented in descending order, from the largest unit at the top, down to the least unit on the grammatical rankscale. Tree diagrams are, therefore, a breakdown of the grammatical categories in the form of a tree growing upside-down. The tree is said to grow upside-down because its root (usually the sentence) grows/points upwards while its branches (usually clauses, phrases, words and morphemes) grow/point downwards. Diagramming in linguistics originated in Traditional Grammar in the form of 'parsing' (Olujide, 1999). Such diagrams, now known as *tree diagrams*, have been modified in many significant ways by modern grammarians such as transformational grammarians (who also call them *phrase markers*) and systemic grammarians. Below are sample tree diagrams in Transformational Generative Grammar (TGG) and Systemic Functional Grammar (SFG) models, using the last example (Pattern 9) of the basic simple sentences above. Note that our aim here is just to familiarize the reader with tree diagrams in syntax and not to explain the processes involved in generating them, as this is outside the purview of this book. To simplify the tree diagrams, a key of symbols used has been provided after each model.

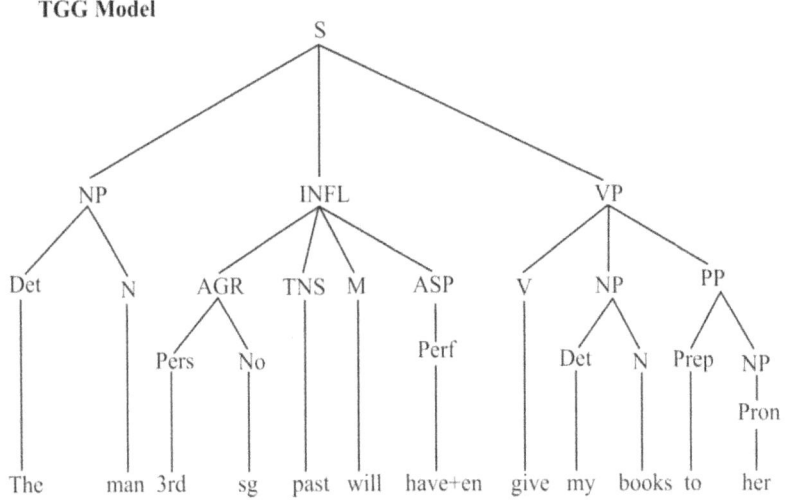

Figure 5: A Sample Tree Diagram in Transformational Generative Grammar

Key to Symbols
S = Sentence
NP = Noun Phrase
Det = Determiner
N = Noun
INFL = Inflection
AGR = Agreement
Pers = Person
No = Number
TNS = Tense
M = Modal
ASP = Aspect
Perf = Perfective
VP = Verb Phrase
V = Verb
PP = Prepositional Phrase
Prep = Preposition
Pron = Pronoun
sg = Singular
3rd = Third (Person)
en = Past Participle

SFG Model

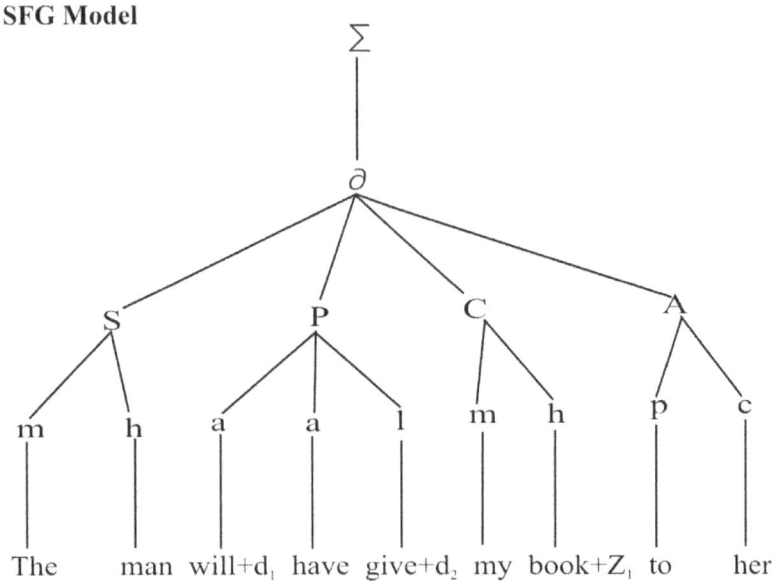

Figure 6: A Sample Tree Diagram in Systemic Functional Grammar

Key to Symbols

Σ = Sigma (Sentence)

∂ = Alpha (Independent Clause)

S = Subject

m = modifier

h = headword

P = Predicate

a = auxiliary

l = lexical

C = Complement

A = Adjunct

p = prepend

c = completive

d_1 = simple past tense

d_2 = past participle

Z_1 = plural

7.6 Grammar and Context

To conclude this chapter, context i.e. a general concept in linguistics, meaning anything 'we need to know about to properly understand the event, action or discourse' (Van Dijk, 1977, in Odebunmi, 2016. p. 13) is a crucial consideration in grammatical interpretation or language use. In fact, any grammatical unit (morpheme, word, phrase, clause or sentence) should be meaningful in the right context or situation of use. This is why any of the other units, apart from the sentence, may as well serve as a (minor) sentence. We shall illustrate this with the following.

X: What is the inflectional morpheme in 'untrue'?

Y: 'Un'. (morpheme)

X: How many siblings have you?

Y: Three. (word)

X: Where do you live?

Y: Down the street. (phrase)

X: What don't you know?

Y: Whether I will come or not. (clause)

The responses of 'Y' to the questions of 'X' above range from a morpheme to a clause. But these responses can also be regarded as sentences (minor sentences) on their own since they are independent and meaningful in their contexts. Besides, note that, like a declarative sentence, each of them starts with a capital letter and ends with a full stop.

Revision Exercise 15

1. Briefly examine the structure of the English sentence with five suitable examples.
2. Discuss the four types of sentences based on function and give two examples of sentences in each case.
3. Structurally speaking, there are four types of English sentences. Expatiate on them, with two examples of each type.
4. Differentiate between major and minor sentences and cite four examples of each.
5. With two examples for each pattern, analyze the patterns of basic simple sentences.
    a. Using either the TGG or SFG approach, draw tree diagrams for any two of the simple sentences that you have cited in (a) above.

PART THREE: ENGLISH GRAMMAR IN USE

Chapter Eight

APPLICATION OF SYNTACTIC RULES

8.1 Active Voice and Passive Voice

In English, there are two ways of talking about something that involves the doer of an action (subject) and the receiver of the action (object). One of the ways is by putting the subject first while the object comes later in a sentence. Such a structure is called 'active voice'. On the other hand, there can be an inversion of these subject-object roles, in which case the object comes first while the subject comes later to have object-subject roles. This kind of construction is called 'passive voice'. Passive structures are made with a 'be' auxiliary verb and a past participle form of a lexical verb (be + pp). The table below describes active and passive voices in different tenses.

Tense	Active Voice	Passive Voice
Simple present	Alex eats my food.	My food is eaten (by Alex).
Present progressive	Alex is eating my food.	My food is being eaten (by Alex).
Present prefect	Alex has eaten my food.	My food has been eaten (by Alex).

Present prefect	Alex has been eating my food.	My food has been being eaten (by Alex). (unusual/rare)
Simple past	Alex ate my food.	My food was eaten (by Alex).
Past progressive	Alex was eating my food.	My food was being eaten (by Alex).
Past perfect progressive	Alex had been eating my food.	My food had been being eaten (by Alex). (unusual/rare)
Simple future	Alex will eat my food.	My food will be eaten (by Alex).
Future progressive	Alex will be eating my food.	My food will be being eaten (by Alex). (unusual/rare)
Future perfect	Alex will have eaten my food.	My food will have been eaten (by Alex).
Future perfect progressive	Alex will have been eating my food	My food will have been being eaten (by Alex). (unusual/rare)

Note that where there are two objects, either of the two objects can come first in passivization:

Active	Passive
Okocha passed *the ball* (dO) to *Kanu*. (iO)	*The ball* (dO) was passed to *Kanu* (iO) by Okocha. OR Kanu (iO) was passed *the ball* (dO) by Okocha.

The parts of the passive sentences enclosed in brackets are optional. Note also that only constructions with transitive verbs can be changed to passives. Passive structures are normally preferred when we wish to shift the focus of what we are saying to the receiver (object) rather than the doer (subject) of the action. In other words, in passive constructions, we emphasize the object and de-emphasize the subject of the sentence.

The subject and object roles explained above have been given different terms in the metalanguages of TGG and SFG. In TGG, they are called 'thematic roles' or 'theta roles' such as: agent, patient, source, goal, instrument, theme, experiencer, etc (Lamidi, 2016, p. 57). In SFG, on the other hand, the clause is first divided into participant, process and circumstance and then, these three roles are further divided into: actor, agent, carrier, material, relational, projecting, etc (Butt, Fahey, Spinks & Yallop, 1995, p. 43).

8.2 Question Tags

    a. You are thirsty, aren't you?

    b. Zion is your sister, isn't she?

    c. Today is not your birthday, is it?

    d. Those ladies have not bathed, have they?

The sentences above, contain two parts each. The first part is a statement whereas the second part is a question, normally called question tag or tag question A question tag is, therefore, a question added to a statement in order to turn it into a question. Question tags are a linguistic device for ensuring cooperation or agreement between speakers and listeners. They are meant to elicit a response from the listener by inviting him/her to agree with you on something.

It is possible to have either a positive/affirmative statement or a negative one. The same goes for a question tag. A positive statement or question tag is one without the adverbial negator 'not' while a negative statement or question tag is one containing 'not'. There are, however, negative words without an overt 'not' such as hardly, seldom, rarely, barely never, etc. These will be discussed fully later. The following are the rules guiding tag questions and responses.

8.2.1 Rules for Question Tags

   i. Positive statement + Negative tag + Positive answer

   ii. Negative statement + Positive tag + Negative answer

The first rule states that a positive statement attracts a negative question tag (such as (a) and (b) above) and then, a positive response. The expected answers to (a) and (b) respectively will thus be:

Yes, I am.

Yes, she is.

The second rule states that a negative statement requires a positive question tag (as exemplified by (c) and (d) above) plus a negative response. Thus, the expected answers to (c) and (d) above are respectively:

No, it isn't.

No, they haven't.

8.2.2 The Structure of Question Tags

Question tags are usually made up of 'an operator and a pronoun subject that echo the operator and subject of the main sentence' (Greenbaum & Nelson, 2009, p. 106). The operator in a tag question is usually an auxiliary verb (be, have, do, will, etc) which is determined by the form (number, tense, etc) of the verb in the statement. The operator is then followed by a pronoun in its subject case (I, he, they, etc) which also reflects the form (number, gender, etc) of the subject of the sentence.

Note also that where the tag is negative, the negator (not) is usually contracted to 'n't' and is part of the operator thus: wasn't, hasn't, didn't, haven't, etc. Note, also, that the contracted form of *am not* is *aren't* NOT **amn't* and that of *I am* is *I'm* NOT **Am* as in: I'm your friend, aren't I? Question tags, as well as contractions, are among the features of speech and informal writing generally called 'colloquialisms'. Other examples are:

Chris can swim, *can't he*?

That boy won the quiz, *didn't he*?

The water wasn't hot, *was it*?

Our lecturer didn't come, *did he*?

It doesn't pay to cheat, *does it*?

1. With covertly negative words (without 'not') such as rarely, seldom, hardly, scarcely, barely, never, etc, positive tag questions are used e.g.

    Dad rarely sleeps late, does he?

    Real men hardly beat women, do they?

    Your former dog never barked at me, did it?

2. Imperatives have various possible tag questions, depending on the mood they express.

    - To invite somebody politely to do something, use 'won't you?' e.g. Sit down, won't you?

- To ask somebody to do something, say 'will/would/can/could you?' e.g. Open the door, will you?
- To express impatience, say 'can't you?' e.g. Keep quiet, can't you?
- Use 'will you' after negative imperatives e.g. Don't speed, will you?
- Others
- After 'let's' used for orders, suggestions, etc, we say 'shall we?' e.g. Let's pray, shall we? Let's dance, shall we?
- In question tags, 'it' is used to refer to 'nothing' and 'everything' e.g. Nothing is hidden, is it? Everything is ready, isn't it?
- 'They' is used to refer to everybody/everyone/somebody/someone/nobody/no one in tag questions e.g. Nobody saw you, did they? Everybody has arrived for the party, haven't they?
- Both 'do' and 'have' are possible in tag questions after the non-auxiliary 'have' e.g. You have a house, haven't/don't you?
- The tag question for 'used to' is 'didn't' as in 'Hassan used to eat egg at childhood, didn't he?'
- 'Same-way' question tags (Swan, 2005, p. 472) follow the pattern of their statements i.e. they are positive or negative as their statements. Such tags usually express interest, surprise, concern, irony, sarcasm, doubt, etc.
- So you're travelling to Britain, are you? (surprise)

- You call that success, do you? (sarcasm)

Note: The phenomenon involved in same-way question tags above is similar to that of *echo questions* in which all or part of a question may be repeated by a hearer to question what has been said by a speaker (Swan, 2005, pp. 467-468). The main difference between them is that unlike same-way question tags, echo questions are not necessarily tagged to statements and can be in a variety of ways thus:

A: I've just secured a new job.

B: You've just secured a new job? OR

B: You've just secured a new what? OR

B: You've just secured what?

Let us round off our discussion on question tags with this general note on answering questions. Different languages have different ways of answering questions. For instance, Nigerian languages such as Yoruba, Igbo and Hausa have a fixed tag question (i.e. ... *abi?* in Yoruba, ... *o 'kwa ya?* in Igbo and ... *ko (ba haka ba)?* in Hausa) for all statements. These question tags correspond to the English ... *is (n't) it?*. This is why many of such learners of English as a Second Language (ESL) tend to tag their statements with ... *isn't it?* even when it is not applicable. The use of all-purpose questions as these 'is common among learners of English as a second or foreign language the world over and ... English is unique among major languages in having reflexive tags and echo questions' (Jowitt, 1991, p. 123).

Likewise, to the question 'Didn't you see me?' the response 'Yes' means 'I saw you' (from the full major sentence 'Yes, I saw you.') while the response 'No' means 'I didn't see you' (from the full major sentence 'No, I didn't see you'), not the other way round. Always ensure that your response does not contradict your intention.

8.3 Direct Speech and Indirect Speech

There are two different ways of talking about what somebody else has said. The first way has to do with giving the exact words of the speaker verbatim (word-for-word). This is called direct speech. In the second style, the speaker's words are made part of our own utterance by effecting changes where necessary. This is known as indirect/reported speech. The difference between the two styles is generally based on the use of tense, pronouns, possessive determiners and words denoting distance and time. Take a look at this:

Speaker: I have a lecture tomorrow.

Direct: She said 'I have a lecture tomorrow.'

Indirect: She said that she had a lecture the following day.

Note that inverted commas/quotation marks are used to enclose the words of the speaker in the direct speech as above and that the quotation marks can either be single (British style) or double (American style).

8.3.1 Use of Tenses

Present tenses in direct speech are changed to past tenses in indirect speech while past tenses in direct speech become past perfect tenses in indirect speech as (1) and (2) below show respectively.

1. Speaker: Today is Monday.

    Direct: He said 'Today is Monday.'

    Indirect: He said that, that day was Monday.

2. Speaker: We gave him some money.

   Direct: Henry said 'We gave him some money.'

   Indirect: Henry said that they had given him some money.

The exception to these rules on tenses is that with situations that have not changed (i.e. if the speaker's present and future tenses remain the same) 'a reporter can often choose whether to keep the original speaker's tenses or to change them, after a past reporting verb' (Swan, 2005, p. 251). This includes situations commonly known as 'universal truths'. According to Swan (2005), the use of a past tense in such a situation is to show that you do not agree with what is said or that you doubt its veracity. Examples:

Direct: The geographer said, 'the sun rises in the east.'

Indirect: The geographer said that the sun rises/rose in the east.

Direct: 'It will rain in the afternoon,' the meteorologist forecast.

Indirect: The meteorologist forecast that it will/would rain in the/that afternoon.

Direct: 'Man is a social animal,' asserted Aristotle.

Indirect: Aristotle asserted that man is/was a social animal.

8.3.2 Use of Pronouns

The table below shows changes in the use of pronouns when we change from direct speech to indirect speech.

Direct speech	Indirect speech	
First Person	Second Person	Third Person
I	you	he/she
me	you	him/her

we	you	they
us	you	them
mine	yours	his/hers
ours	yours	theirs
myself	yourself	himself/herself
ourselves	yourselves	themselves

Example

Direct: William confessed 'I myself did the work.'

Indirect: William confessed that he had done the work himself.

8.3.3 Use of Determiners

Direct Speech	Indirect Speech
my	his/her
our	their
your	my/our
his	his
her	her
their	their

Example

Direct: 'Treat my children as your own,' Mrs Wura urged me.

Indirect: Mrs Wura urged me to treat her children as my own.

8.3.4 Use of Words Denoting Distance and Time

While reporting speeches, words denoting nearness are changed to corresponding words denoting remoteness in space and time.

Direct speech	Indirect speech
this	That
these	Those
now	Then

ago	Before
here	There
soon	Later
today	that day
tonight	that night
tomorrow	the next day/the following day
the next day	the following day/the day after
yesterday	the previous day/the day before
last night	the previous night/the night before

Example

Direct Speech: Yemi said 'I saw this book here yesterday.'

Indirect Speech: Yemi said that he had seen that book there the previous day.

8.3.5 Indirect Speech and the Sentence Types

Different sentence types undergo different changes while converting them from direct to reported speech. One of these changes is in the use of reporting verbs. A reporting verb is one that introduces a reported speech. We shall see this more clearly shortly.

Indirect Speech and Declarative Sentences

To change declarative sentences to reported speech, the following rules are important.

a. The reporting verb is usually 'said' or 'told' (me/you/him/them, etc). Other verbs such as answered, stated, disclosed, declared, informed, etc are also possible, depending on the import or meaning of the statement e.g.

   Direct: 'The plane will soon arrive,' he said.

   Indirect: He announced/informed us that the plane would later arrive.

b. The conjunction 'that' sometimes comes after the reporting verb while reporting declarative sentences e.g.

   Direct: The nanny said 'The baby has eaten.'

   Indirect: The nanny said that the baby had eaten.

Indirect Speech and Interrogative Sentences

The following rules are applicable when reporting questions.

a. Usually, the reporting verb is 'asked' but others such as inquired, requested, questioned, demanded, wanted to know, etc may also be used e.g.

   Direct: 'How old are you?' asked the teacher.

   Indirect: The teacher asked/wanted to know how old the pupil was.

b. 'Whether' or 'if' is sometimes placed after the reporting verb e.g.

   Direct: The doctor asked 'Are you okay now?'

   Indirect: The doctor asked/wanted to know if I was okay then.

c. Remove the question mark to change the question to a statement.

Indirect Speech and Imperative Sentences

a. The usual reporting verbs for imperative sentences are commanded, ordered, requested, begged, entreated, solicited, etc as in:

Direct: 'Get out!' he ordered.

Indirect: He ordered them (to get) out.

b. Remove the exclamation mark, if there is any, to change the sentence to a statement.

Indirect Speech and Exclamatory Sentences

a. Exclamations are usually reported with the verb 'exclaimed'. Others such as 'shouted', congratulated, wished, etc may also be used e.g.

Direct: 'Congratulations on your promotion!' Obi said to Eze.

Indirect: Obi congratulated Eze on his promotion.

b. Exclamatory markers such as 'what', 'how', 'oh', 'hurray', 'wow', etc are removed from reported exclamations e.g.

Direct: 'Oh! What a brilliant suggestion you've got!' my boss told me.

Indirect: My boss exclaimed with excitement that I had got a brilliant suggestion.

c. The exclamation mark (!) is removed from reported exclamatory sentences. (See the examples above.)

8.4 Conditional Sentences

a. If he goes to school, he will be a professor.

b. If he went to school, he would be a professor.

c. If he had gone to school, he would have been a professor.

Conditional sentences are sentences like those above which express the dependence of one circumstance on another. A conditional sentence is a complex sentence that is made up of two clauses - one dependent and another independent or vice versa - 'with a fixed sequence of tenses' (Whitebread & Ajayi, 2012, p. 49). By 'a fixed sequence of tenses', is meant that the two clauses in the conditional sentence must be in the same tense. You may wish to refer to our earlier discussion on 'Sequence of Tenses'.

In many cases, conditional sentences are introduced by dependent if-clauses as in (a) to (c) above but in other cases, there is a reversal, thus fronting the independent clause as in 'He will be a professor if he goes to school'. It is also possible for the conjunction 'if' not to start the dependent clause in a conditional sentence e.g. Had he gone to school, he would have been a professor. There are three kinds of conditional sentences in English, these are: first conditional, second conditional and third conditional (Swan, 2005, p. 233) which are respectively exemplified by sentences (a), (b) and (c) above. We shall examine them in turn.

8.4.1 First Conditionals/Open Conditions/Real Conditions

These describe conditions which may or may not be fulfilled or situations which may not happen, thus leaving open the fulfilment of such conditions. First conditionals can either be in present or past tenses referring to present or past situations. The structure of first conditionals is: present if-clause + present main clause OR past if-clause + past main clause (or vice versa).

a. If I *travel* to Dubai I *will* buy gold.

b. Mummy *may* like it if she *sees* it.

c. If you *make* (a) noise, you *will* be punished.

d. If Yinka *came* to school yesterday, then, he *broke* the louvres.

e. He certainly *left* the gate open, if he *entered* last.

8.4.2 Second Conditionals/Closed Conditions/Unreal Conditions

They describe imaginary or improbable conditions which, expectedly, will not be fulfilled. Past tenses are used in unreal conditions 'to distance our language from reality' (Swan, 2005, p. 234). The structure of second conditionals is: past if-clause + past main clause or vice versa.

a. If I *were* a woman, I *would* remain a virgin till I married. (said by a man)

b. I *would* help the poor if I *were* rich. (but I'm not rich)

c. If I *won* this election, I *could* be a millionaire. (said by the least popular candidate)

d. *Were* it cold/if it *were* cold, the meat *would* not rot. (but it is hot)

Note that the use of 'were' instead of 'was' after 'if' as we have in (a) and (d) above is grammatically known as 'subjunctive' (mood).

8.4.3 Third Conditionals/Unfulfilled Conditions

They tell us that something did not happen because a certain condition was not fulfilled. Third conditionals have the structure: past perfect if-clause + past participle main clause or vice versa.

a. If Seun *had worked* harder, he *would have come* first.
b. The man *might have won* the election if he *had contested*.
c. *Had* she *eaten* the food, she *would have died*.
d. *Would*n't they *have succeeded* if they *had been encouraged*?

What (a) means is that Seun did not come first because he did not work hard enough while (b) means that the man did not win the election because he did not contest.

Note that it is wrong to alter the tense pattern of the conditionals, especially in British English. Hence, it is wrong to say, for instance:

*If I *travel* (present) to Dubai, I *would* (past) buy gold.

*I *would have helped* (past participle) the poor if I *were* (past tense) rich.

*If Godwin *had worked* (past perfect) harder, he *will* (present) come first.

However, in American English, a past tense is sometimes used instead of a past perfect tense in the if-clause of third conditionals thus: If she *ate* (past) the food she *would have died*.

8.5 Concord in English

Concord in grammar refers to correspondence or agreement between the elements of a sentence. Concord is traditionally called 'agreement' because the parts of the sentence concerned are said to 'agree'. Consider:

a. The bird flies high.
b. The birds fly high.
c. *The bird fly high.

d. *The birds flies high.

In (a) and (b) above, there is agreement between the subject and the verb because in (a) the singular subject (bird) is used with a corresponding singular verb (flies) and in (b), the plural subject (birds) goes with the plural verb (fly). On the other hand, there is a mismatch in (c) where a singular subject (bird) is used with a plural verb (fly) and in (d) where a plural subject (birds) co-occurs with a singular verb (flies). This mismatch is an error of concord which is why (c) and (d) are wrong.

One of the areas of problem to learners of English as a Second Language in concord is the inability to differentiate between singular and plural nouns and verbs. To solve this, note that most singular nouns do not end in 's'(e.g. bird, uncle, city, etc) but most singular verbs do (e.g. flies, washes, speaks, etc). On the contrary, most plural nouns end in 's' while most plural verbs do not (e.g. fly, wash, speak, etc)

Apart from 'was' and 'were' which are the respective singular past and plural past forms of the verb 'be', concord rules are only applicable to verbs in their present tenses. However, concord rules are not applicable to the modals because they do not show number. Grammarians such as Quirk and Greenbaum (1973), Leech and Svartvik (2012), and Greenbaum and Nelson (2009) have classified concord variously. This is summarized below.

8.5.1 Subject-Verb Concord: This refers to agreement in number between the subject and the verb in a sentence. In English, a singular subject takes a singular verb while a plural subject takes a plural verb. Subject-verb concord is the broadest and the most prominent type of concord in English.

The food (S) *tastes* (V) nice.

Do (V) *your children* (S) bath in the morning during harmattan?

Clauses and phrases used as subject attract singular verbs even if they contain plural nouns e.g.

What he gained from the business deals (S) *was* (V) meager.

Before dawn (S) *is* (V) my best reading time.

Subject-verb concord can be sub-divided into the following.

1. **Concord with Coordinated Subjects:** This is concord involving the coordinating conjunction 'and' used to join two or more nouns together. When the coordinated subjects refer to separate things, a plural verb is used:

   Ibukun and her brother (S) have (V) a bicycle.

   However, with appositional subjects (also joined by 'and') the choice of the verb is determined by the number of either of the two conjoined subjects because, of course, both subjects are either singular or plural e.g.

   His wife and mother (S) of his two children is (V) dead.

   Bread and tea (S) was (V) taken for breakfast.

   Your new dress and pride (S) provokes/provoke (V) him.

   In cases of ambiguity such as the last example above, context determines whether a singular or plural verb should be used. For instance, if the new dress is also the person's pride (what he/she is proud of), a singular verb should be used but if the dress and the pride (an attitude) are seen as two separate entities, a plural verb should be used.

2. **Concord with Quasi-coordinators:** Quasi-coordinators are conjunctions such as with, together with, in conjunction with, in addition to, as well as, as much as, like, etc which look like the coordinator 'and' but are not used as it is used. With quasi-coordinators, the first noun

is the main subject and it always determines the status of the verb. In other words, a singular first noun requires a singular verb and a plural first noun requires a plural verb. In each of the following sentences, the first noun and the verb are italicized.

Raymond (S) together with his missing sisters *has* (V) been found.

The teacher (S) as well as the pupils *is* (V) to blame for the failure.

The quintuplets (S), like their mother, *are* (V) healthy.

Those lorries (S) in addition to that helicopter *belong* (V) to him.

3. **Concord with Pluralia Tantum:** Pluralia tantum are words that always appear in plural form (with the suffix '-s'). They may, however, be used as singular or plural. Hence, there are two categories of pluralia tantum. (For a comprehensive list of both types, see the section on number category in nouns.) Many students tend to use singular pluralia tantum including games/sports (e.g. dominoes), diseases (e.g. rabies), school subjects (e.g. economics) and others (e.g. news) as plural, thus, committing errors of concord.

Rabies (S) *has* (V) been eradicated with the killing of the dogs.

Linguistics (S) *is* (V) interesting.

The news (S) of his arrest *spreads* (V) like wild fire.

Windows (S) *is* (V) an operating system that controls a personal computer.

4. **Concord with Mathematical Expressions:** The following computations can either take a singular or plural verb e.g.

   Two and four (S) is/are (V) six.

   One plus one (S) does/do (V) not always make two.

   However, the choice of the verb depends on whether the main noun or pronoun subject (in italics here) is singular or plural in the following expressions of fraction and percentage.

   Half of the *refugees* (S) are (V) children.

   Three quarters of the *job* (S) has (V) been done.

   Ten percent of *it* (S) goes (V) to charity.

   Sixty percent of the *candidates* (S) were (V) successful.

5. **Concord with Units of Measurement:** When units of measurement such as time, distance, length, weight and money have plural modifiers (e.g. three weeks, twenty miles, five million naira, etc), they have the notion of a single entity and so, they take singular verbs.

   Four months *was* too short to complete the building.

   Ten billion dollars *has* been allocated for the project.

   Note that when the unit is not specified numerically, a plural verb is used (Ojo, 2011) as in:

   Several months *were* spent on the building. ('Several' is not specific.)

   Billions of dollars *have* been allocated for the project. ('Billions' is not specific.)

6. **Concord with Quotations and Titles:** Quotations and titles are generally regarded as singular even if they contain plural nouns. Hence, singular verbs are used with them e.g.

Twenty Friends in twenty Years (S) was (V) the title of the movie.

The Lion and the Jewel (S) is (V) Wole Soyinka's masterpiece.

7. **Notional Concord:** In the words of Quirk and Greenbaum (1973, p. 176), 'Notional concord' is the agreement of verb with subject according to the idea of number rather than the actual presence of the grammatical marker for that idea.' This occurs in situations where there is no –s inflection to show plurality in words. A word's singularity or plurality is, therefore, determined by the concept it represents.

Collective nouns such as family, audience, committee, public, class, team, government, etc are affected by the principle of notional concord. In British English, such nouns as in the examples below are notionally plural and require plural verbs. On the other hand, in American English, they are singular and so, they attract singular verbs.

The *team* (S) *are* (V) quarrelling about the money.

His family (S) *have* (V) just arrived from Lagos.

The committee (S) *have* (V) agreed on the matter.

However, the overriding consideration in the choice of a verb depends on whether the group is seen as one indivisible entity in which case a singular verb is used or it is viewed as a collection of individuals acting or reacting separately to a phenomenon in which a plural verb is used. Consider, for example, the following sentence where a singular verb is used.

The team (S) is (V) united.

His family (S) is (V) the most famous in the United States.

The committee (S) has (V) submitted its report.

8. **Proximity Concord:** Also called 'attraction', proximity is a principle in concord whereby the verb agrees with the noun or pronoun that comes closely before it. Hence, if the noun or pronoun is singular, a singular verb is used while a plural verb is used if it is plural. Note that the noun or noun phrase which determines the status of the verb is italicized in addition to the verb in the examples following the rules below.

First and foremost, two or more nouns or pronouns joined by the coordinating conjunction 'or' obey the proximity principle e.g.

Three teenagers or *one adult* (S) *is* (V) enough for the work.

Likewise, when a correlative conjunction such as 'either... or', 'neither... nor', 'not only... but also', etc is used to join two subjects, the principle of proximity concord is applied e.g.

Either the bag or *the shoes* (S) *were* (V) sold by her.

Neither her criticisms nor *her commendation* (S) *makes* (V) sense to me.

Also, indefinite pronouns such as 'nobody', 'everyone', 'everything' and determiners such as 'no', 'every', 'each', etc, obey the proximity principle (Quirk & Greenbaum, 1973, p. 179).

Every *man* (S) *has* (V) a cutlass in the village.

None of *them* (S) *know* (V) me.

Either of the *guests* (S) *are* (V) welcome.

Note that it is the italicized subjects that determine the verbs in the examples above. However, in formal contexts, singular verbs are preferred with such pronouns.

The phrase 'a number of', when used with a subject, attracts a plural verb in line with the proximity rule e.g.

A number of *cows* (S) *were* grazing on the field.

Finally, here, the phrase 'many a' which is normally used with a singular subject, goes with a singular verb, in accordance with the principle of proximity.

Many a *lady* (S) *wishes* (V) to marry a wealthy guy.

9. **Concord of Person:** This is agreement between the first, second and third persons in English pronouns and their verb forms, such that it will be wrong to interchange the pronouns or verbs indiscriminately.

   First Person: *I* (S) *am* (V) fine.

   Second Person: *You* (S) *are* (V) fine.

   Third Person: *He* (S) *is* (V) fine.

   Likewise, when relative pronouns such as who, that, which, etc come between the (pronoun) subject and the verb, the verb agrees in number and person with the subject:

   It's *I* (S) who *am* (V) calling you (I am ...)

   It's *you* (S) that *are* (V) not serious. (You are ...)

   It's *she* (S) who *is* (V) to go (She is ...)

8.5.2 Subject-Complement Concord: This kind of agreement occurs between the subject (S) of the sentence and its complement (C) in terms of number. Hence, a singular subject is followed by a singular complement and a plural subject by a plural complement thus:

That boy (S) is a genius (C). (Not 'geniuses')

Those boys (S) are geniuses (C). (Not 'a genius')

But this is not applicable to the following sentences where plural subjects take corresponding singular objects:

Children (S) are a blessing (C) to their parents.

Mr and Mrs Allan (S) are a wonderful couple (C).

8.5.3 Subject-Object Concord: This takes place between the subject (S) and the object (O) in a sentence in terms of number, person and gender e.g.

Vivian (S) bit *herself* (O) while eating.

They (S) like *themselves* (O) to a fault.

The actors (S) have taken off *their costume* (O).

8.5.4 Pronoun-Antecedent Concord: When used formally, indefinite pronouns such as everybody, everyone, somebody, someone, anybody, anyone, nobody and no one are replaced by the third person singular pronoun 'he', or its equivalent as in Everybody (Antec) knows that he (Pron) must die. Another formal but awkward alternative is to use 'he or she' or its equivalent thus: Everybody (Antec) knows that he or she (Pron) must die. On the other hand, in informal usage, to avoid the sexist bias of the first style above and the awkwardness of the second style, the third person plural pronoun 'they' or its equivalent is used as in: Everybody (Antec) knows that they (Pron) must die.

8.5.5 Determiner-Antecedent Concord: It is agreement between the third person determiners (Det) and their antecedents (Antec) on the basis of number and gender e.g.

Caleb (Antec) cut *his* (Det) finger nails.

The girl (Antec) helps *her* (Det) mother.

Those traders (Antec) have lost *their* (Det) money.

Revision Exercise 16

1. Change these sentences from active to passive voice.
   a. They are reading Shakespeare's The Tempest.
   b. He takes lemon juice and honey regularly.
   c. Diana cut the vegetables.
   d. The man was buying a newspaper.
   e. We should have accepted the offer.
2. Supply the tag questions to these statements and imperatives.
   a. I am late, ... ?
   b. You didn't eat last night, ... ?
   c. Let's go, ... ?
   d. Close your eyes, ... ?
   e. Stand upright, ... ?
   f. Don't make a noise, ... ?
   g. Azeez rarely fights with anyone, ... ?
   h. Somebody has changed my seat, ... ?
   i. The doctor used to come here, ... ?
   j. That man hasn't a daughter, ... ?
3. Convert the following structures from direct to indirect speech.

a. My friend said 'I will see you soon.'
b. The businessman said 'My order arrived yesterday.'
c. Victor asked 'How old are you?'
d. 'We only came here over an hour ago' they confessed.
e. Mum exclaimed 'Wow! How excellent your result is!'

4. Choose from the given options to complete these sentences.
   a. If the man were a governor, he ... scholarships. (a) will award (b) would have awarded (c) would award (d) awards
   b. If she succeeds, she ... happy. (a) will be (b) would have been (c) would be (d) could be
   c. Had we known his lazy attitude, we ... him. (a) would not employ (b) should not employ (c) will not have employed (d) would not have employed
   d. If I ... God, rain would not fall on the farms of sinners. (a) am (b) may be (c) were (d) had been
   e. If Joseph ... the wine, he would have been poisoned. (a) takes (b) took (c) has taken (d) had taken

5. From the given options, choose the most suitable verb to complete each sentence.
   a. That they complain of insufficient funds **is/are** ridiculous.
   b. Rice and beans **is/are** his best food.
   c. The teacher together with the students **has/have** gone on an excursion.

d. Athletics **keep/keeps** you fit.
e. Two third of the victims of the inferno **was/were** children.
f. The audience **is/are** quarreling about the outcome of the programme.
g. Either the house or the shops **is/are** to be demolished.
h. None of those spoons **has/have** been washed.
i. A large number of turkeys **was/were** slaughtered for the wedding.
a. Many a man **likes/like** to marry a beautiful woman.

Chapter Nine

COMMON ERRORS IN ENGLISH GRAMMAR

9.1 Error or Mistake?

Errors are instances of deviation from the acceptable norm or standard of a particular language. Technically speaking, errors are different from mistakes, otherwise called 'slips'. The major difference between errors and mistakes is that errors are not self-identifiable nor self-correctable but mistakes are (Crystal, 2015). Grammatical errors are very common among second language learners of English for so many reasons. One of these reasons is the already acquired structure of their first language (L1) or mother tongue (MT) which conflicts with the structure of English. Some errors have already been identified and explained in the course of discussing relevant topics in this book. However, we have devoted this chapter to treating common errors to give them the necessary attention and correct them. The errors are divided into two: morphological errors and syntactic errors.

9.2 Morphological Errors

These are errors that relate to the use of morphemes and individual words as we discussed in Part One of this book with the title 'Morphology'. The words in a language are classified, based on their functions, into parts of speech or word classes and we have used the same classification for our morphological errors.

9.2.1 Errors Relating to the Use of Nouns

1. **Wrong**: The woman gave *an advice* to her wedding daughter.

   Right: The woman gave *advice/a piece of advice* to her wedding daughter.

2. **Wrong**: *Slangs* are very common among adolescents today.

   Right: *Slang* is very common among adolescents today.

   Right: *Slang expressions* are very common among adolescents today.

Note: Nouns such as 'advice', 'slang', 'furniture', 'news', 'equipment', 'paper', 'luggage', etc are mass or uncountable nouns. Do not use the indefinite articles ('a' or 'an') or the plural marker ('s') with them. (See the section on 'Countable and Uncountable Nouns' for more.)

3. **Wrong**: He is a *staff* of Shell Petroleum Company of Nigeria.

   Right: He is a *member of staff* of Shell Petroleum Company of Nigeria.

   Right: He is a *staffer* of Shell Petroleum Company of Nigeria. (AmE)

4. **Wrong**: I know all the *terminologies* in linguistics.

   Right: I know all the *terminology/terms* in linguistics.

5. **Wrong**: The groom bought expensive *clothings* for his bride.

   Right: The groom bought expensive *clothing/clothes* for his bride.

Note: Nouns such as 'staff', 'terminology', 'clothing', 'bedding', 'machinery' and 'jewellery' (BrE) or 'jewelry' (AmE) are collective nouns which are already notionally plural. Pluralizing them with 's' or 'ies', or singularizing them with 'a' or 'an' is, therefore, wrong.

6. **Wrong**: I bought my car *plate number* from Lagos State.

   Right: I bought my car *number plate* from Lagos State.

Note: In 'number plate', 'number' is the adjective which should qualify the noun 'plate' and not the other way round. In American English, 'number plate' is called 'license plate'. Similarly, 'driving licence' is British English while 'driver's license' is American English. Also, note the difference in the spelling of the word 'licence' (BrE) and 'license' (AmE).

7. **Wrong**: My brother is an *academician* because he is a lecturer.

   Right: My brother is an *academic* because he is a lecturer.

8. **Wrong**: The company organized a *send-forth* for the outgoing manager.

   Right: The company organized a *send-off* for the outgoing manager.

9. **Wrong**: He is the new chairman of the *parents'-teachers' association*.

   Right: He is the new chairman of the *parent-teacher association*.

10. **Wrong**: One of the *corpers* is an engineer.

    Right: One of the *corps members* is an engineer.

Note: 'Corps' is pronounced /kɔ:/. The letters 'p' and 's' are silent in the word.

9.2.2 Errors Relating to the Use of Adjectives

1. **Wrong**: Nelson is your *junior* brother, isn't he?

    Right: Nelson is your *younger* brother, isn't he?

2. **Wrong**: The girl is *plumpy* and pretty.

    Right: The girl is *plump* and pretty.

Note: 'Plumpy' is not an English word.

3. **Wrong**: She is a *matured* young girl.

    Right: She is a *mature* young girl.

Note: The word 'matured' is a verb i.e. the past tense of 'mature' as in 'She has *matured* a great deal over the past year'. The adjective form is 'mature', as we have in the right sentence above. The same explanation is applicable to 'secure' and 'secured'.

4. **Wrong**: My table is *more higher* than yours.

    Right: My table is *higher* than yours.

5. **Wrong**: I have a *running* nose.

    Right: I have a *runny* nose.

6. **Wrong**: My wife is *heavy*.

    Right: My wife is *pregnant*.

7. **Wrong**: His result was *very excellent*.

Right: His result was *excellent*.

Note: Adjectives such as 'excellent', 'perfect', etc cannot be intensified with 'very' because there is no degree of excellence, perfection, etc. (See 'Absolute Adjectives' for more of such adjectives.)

8. **Wrong**: The tortoise is a *trickish* animal.

   Right: The tortoise is a *tricky* animal.

9. **Wrong**: Many of the female students in that school are *indisciplined*.

   Right: Many of the female students in that school are *undisciplined*.

10. **Wrong**: Eze travelled to Onitsha on a *luxurious* bus.

    Right: Eze travelled to Onitsha on a *luxury* bus.

9.2.3 Errors Relating to the Use of Verbs

1. **Wrong**: How many of the candidates *scaled* through?

   Right: How many of the candidates *sailed* through?

2. **Wrong**: We are not *hearing* you; speak louder.

   Right: We *cannot hear* you; speak louder.

Note: Verbs such as 'hear', 'see', 'understand', 'know', etc cannot be used in the progressive tense. For more on this, see the section on 'Stative Verbs'.

3. **Wrong**: Please, *borrow* me your ruler.

   Right: Please, *lend* me your ruler.

Note: To 'borrow' is to 'collect' but to 'lend' is to 'give'.

4. **Wrong**: Joshua *cracked* his brain(s) for the solution to the problem.

   Right: Joshua *racked* his brain(s) for the solution to the problem.

5. **Wrong**: *Should in case* you travel to Kano, buy me some fabrics.

   Right: *Should* you travel to Kano, buy me some fabrics.

   Right: *In case* you travel to Kano, buy me some fabrics.

6. **Wrong**: I will *write* an exam at 8am tomorrow.

   Right: I will *sit (for)/take/do* an exam at 8am tomorrow.

Note: While 'take' is generally used in both British English and American English, 'sit' is used in British English and 'sit for' in American English for examinations, tests and the like (NOT 'and the *likes'). On the other hand, 'do' is British English.

7. **Wrong**: It *doesn't* worth fighting in public.

   Right: It *isn't* worth fighting in public.

8. **Wrong**: You *suppose* to know better than this.

   Right: You *are supposed* to know better than this.

9. **Wrong**: Anita *must have to* work harder this time.

   Right: Anita *must* work harder this time.

   Right: Anita *has to* work harder this time.

Note: 'Must' and 'have to' are synonymous. Use only one of them at a time.

10. **Wrong**: The girl was *disvirgined* by her boyfriend.

    Right: The girl was *deflowered* by her boyfriend.

Note: Even though 'virgin' is an English word, 'disvirgin' is not. The prefix 'dis' added to the word is, therefore, a pseudo-morpheme. Learn more about pseudo-morphemes in Chapter Two.

9.2.4 Errors Relating to the Use of Adverbs

1. **Wrong**: The rain has not stopped *self*.

    Right: The rain has not stopped *even*. OR *Even,* the rain has not stopped. OR The rain has not *even* stopped.

Note: The word 'self' is not an adverb but a noun and, therefore, it cannot modify a verb such as 'stopped' in the wrong example above. Adverbs are mobile, as shown by the different positions of 'even' in the alternative correct structures but 'self' cannot be so used.

2. **Wrong**: We will pay the arrears *instalmentally*.

    Right: We will pay the arrears *in/by instalments*.

Note: There is no word as 'instalmentally' in English.

3. **Wrong**: Can you say the national anthem *off-head*?

    Right: Can you say the national anthem *offhand/by heart*?

4. **Wrong**: *Kindly* help me to lift the load. (As a polite request)

    Right: *Please* help me to lift the load. (As a polite request)

Note: 'Kindly' is not synonymous with 'please'. While 'please' is used in making polite requests, 'kindly' suggests annoyance and impatience. Hence, it is impolite.

5. **Wrong**: He ate *too* much *that* he could not even stand up.

Right: He ate *so* much *that* he could not even stand up.

Right: He ate *too* much *to* even stand up.

Note: The adverb 'too' goes with 'to' while 'so' goes with 'that'. Check the chapter on adverbs for details on this'

6. **Wrong**: We have been waiting for you *since*.

   Right: We have been waiting for you *since 10am*.

   Right: We have been waiting for you *for a long time*.

Note: 'Since' cannot stand alone as an adverb of time.

7. **Wrong**: I have been here for two hours *ago*.

   Right: I have been here for two hours *now*.

8. **A**: Do you care for some coffee?

   B: **(Wrong)** No, *please*.

   B: **(Right)** No, *thanks*.

   B: **(Righ**t) Yes, *please*.

Note: The adverb '"Please' cannot follow 'No'" (to reject an offer), "it can only follow 'Yes'" (to accept it) (Jowitt & Nnamonu, 1985, p. 106).

9. **Wrong**: The oil will not be enough for us. *So therefore*, go and buy your own.

   Right: The oil will not be enough for us. *So*, go and buy your own.

   Right: The oil will not be enough for us. *Therefore*, go and buy your own.

Note: 'So' and 'therefore' are synonymous and so, they should not follow each other.

10. **Wrong**: Although the test was difficult, *yet* she managed to pass it

    Right: Although the test was difficult, she managed to pass it.

Note: Do not follow 'although' or 'though' with the adverb 'yet'.

9.2.5 Errors Relating to the Use of Pronouns

1. **Wrong**: Abdul and Hassan always fight *themselves*.

   Right: Abdul and Hassan always fight *each other*.

2. **Wrong**: *Everybody have* returned from the farm.

   Right: *Everybody has* returned from the farm.

Note: Indefinite pronouns such as 'everybody', 'everything', etc. are used with singular verbs. See the section on 'proximity concord' for more.

3. **A**: Whose money is this?

   B: (**Wrong**) It's *for me*.

   B: (**Right**) It's *mine*.

4. **Wrong**: My sister *she* is a journalist.

   Right: My sister is a journalist.

5. **Wrong**: They do not talk to one another *of which it* is a bad attitude.

   Right: They do not talk to one another *which* is a bad attitude.

Note: The use of the pronoun 'she' in (4) above is redundant. Likewise, the use of, 'of' with the pronoun 'which' and the use of the pronoun 'it' in (5) above is redundant.

6. **Father**: Who is at the door?

   Son: (**Wrong**) It's *I*.

   Son: (**Right**) It's *me*.

Note: The first response above is wrong because it is 'formal and unnatural'. It should, therefore, be avoided in informal 'conversations and ordinary speech' such as we have above (Eyisi, 2015, p. 279). The wrong example is characteristic of Traditional Grammar – an attempt to impose the structures and features of Greek and Latin on English.

7. **Wrong**: He called you and *I*.

   Right: He called you and *me*.

Note: To know the correct pronoun, remove the first object 'you' and the coordinator 'and'. What you have left is:

He called me. (Of course, it is NOT *'He called I')

8. **Wrong**: Adegoke and *her* did the work.

   Right: Adegoke and *she* did the work.

To know the correct pronoun here, remove the first subject and the coordinator ('Adegoke and') and you have:

She did the work. (NOT *'Her did the work')

9. **Wrong**: Faith and *us* are late.

   Right: Faith and *we* are late.

Note: For this, simply remove 'Faith and' to have:

We are late. (Instead of *'Us are late')

10. **Right**: I am older than *she*. (Formal)

    Right: I am older than *her*. (Informal)

Note: Either of these two expressions is acceptable, depending on whether the context of use is formal or informal (Swan, 2005, p. 116; Leech & Svartvik, 2012, pp. 272-273). Saying that the second sentence is wrong, as some people do, therefore, amounts to *hypercorrection*.

9.2.6 Errors Relating to the Use of Prepositions

1. **Wrong:** The school authorities discussed *about* the last riot.

    Right: The school authorities discussed the last riot.

2. **Wrong**: Our committee comprises *of* four men and two women.

    Right: Our committee *comprises* four men and two women.

    Right: Our committee *is comprised of* four men and two women.

Note: The verb 'discuss' as in (1) above does not attract a preposition when used. Likewise, when the verb 'comprise' as in (2) is used in its active form, it does not require a preposition. Only in its passive form, as in the second right sentence above, is a preposition required.

3. **Wrong**: A politician has tested positive *to* coronavirus.

    Right: A politician has tested positive *for* coronavirus.

Note: A person can only test positive or negative *for* a disease/illness, not *to* it because medical tests are meant to test *for* (not *to*) the presence or absence of diseases/illnesses in the body.

4. **Wrong**: Gold is superior *than* silver.

    Right: Gold is superior *to* silver.

Note: 'Superior' is not a comparative like 'younger', 'more careful', etc and it should, therefore, not take 'than'. Likewise, 'prefer' should not be used with 'than' e.g. not *'I prefer tea *than* coffee' but 'I prefer tea *to* coffee'. Only comparatives and few other words such as 'rather' and 'other', are used with the preposition 'than' in English.

5. **Wrong**: The accused was charged *for* manslaughter.

    Right: The accused was charged *with* manslaughter.

6. **Wrong**: Most children in the village go to school *by* feet.

    Right: Most children in the village go to school *on* foot.

7. **Wrong**: He boasts of owning a house *at* Abuja.

    Right: He boasts of owning a house *in* Abuja.

Note: Names of small places such as small towns, areas of a town, villages, streets, hamlets, etc attract 'at' while names of big places such as local government areas, cities, states, countries, continents, etc take 'in'.

8. **Wrong**: Let me congratulate you *for* your success in the exam.

    Right: Let me congratulate you *on* your success in the exam.

9. **Wrong**: We shall order *for* more copies of the book from Ibadan.

    Right: We shall *order* more copies of the book from Ibadan.

Note: When 'order' is used as a verb, it does not take the preposition 'of' but when it is used as a noun, as in the example below, 'for' can follow it.

We have placed an order for more copies of the book from Ibadan.

   10. **Wrong**: I ran into an old friend *in* the plane.

       Right: I ran into an old friend *on* the plane.

Note: When we talk about public transport involving buses, lorries, trains, aeroplanes, ships, etc, 'on' should be used, not 'in'. However, 'in' is used, not 'on', when we talk of queues or lines and motion as in:

Who is the last person *in* the queue? (Not 'on the queue').

The crime suspect jumped out when the car was *in* motion. (Not 'on motion')

9.2.7 Errors Relating to the Use of Conjunctions

   1. **Wrong**: He has eyes *and* cannot see.

      Right: He has eyes *but* cannot see.

   2. **Wrong**: Although he took off last *but* he won the race.

      Right: Although he took off last, he won the race.

Note: Do not follow 'though' or 'although' with the conjunction 'but'.

   3. **Wrong**: *Either* he agrees or not, I will do it.

      Right: *Whether* he agrees or not, I will do it.

   4. **Wrong**: She brushed her teeth *still yet* they smelled.

      Right: She brushed her teeth, *yet* they smelled.

   5. **Right**: She brushed her teeth, *still* they smelled.

Note: 'Still' and 'yet' are adversative coordinators which should not be combined together.

6. **Wrong**: You have no option *than* to apologize.

    Right: You have no option *but* to apologize.

Note: The expression 'no option but' is fixed. Likewise, say 'nothing but' (not 'nothing than') as in: *Nothing but* the truth will save you. Conversely, 'other' collocates with 'than', not 'but' as in: I have no *other* father *than* you.

7. **Wrong**: He asked me *that* where could he get decent food to buy.

    Right: He asked me where he could get decent food to buy.

8. **Wrong**: They did not only pray, they fasted.

    Right: They did not only pray, *but* (they) *also* fasted.

Note: The correlative conjunction 'not only ... but also' should be used together.

9. **Wrong**: *Neither* Ramson will sleep *nor* allow others to sleep.

    Right: Ramson will *neither* sleep *nor* allow others to sleep.

10. **Wrong**: The rainy season is between June *to* August in this area.

    Right: The rainy season is between June *and* August in this area.

    Right: The rainy season is *from* June *to* August in this area.

Note: The preposition 'between' always goes with the conjunction 'and' in structures such as above. Alternatively, you may use 'from ... to' as in the second right sentence.

11. **Wrong**: *Because* he was ill, *so* he couldn't walk.

Right: *Because* he was ill, he couldn't walk.

Right: He was ill, *so* he couldn't walk.

Note: Do not use more than one conjunction to link up two clauses in a sentence. 'Because' is a subordinating conjunction while 'so' is a connective adverb. They both perform linking functions and this is why the first sentence above is wrong.

9.2.8 Errors Relating to the Use of Determiners

1. **Wrong**: Add five marks across board.

   Right: Add five marks across *the* board.

Note: Like the above example, it is wrong to leave out 'the' in 'get the cane' (be punished with a cane) and 'be in the money' (rich) as in:

You will get *the* cane if you don't behave (yourself).

Mike, my old classmate, is now in *the* money.

2. **Wrong**: I warned *the both* of them.

   Right: I warned *both* of them.

Note: 'Both' means 'the two'. Since 'the' is already implied in the meaning, adding another 'the' is tautological and, therefore, wrong. Even though 'the' should not precede 'both', it may come after 'both' as in: *Both (the)* boys are funny.

3. **Wrong**: Barcelona is *an* European football club.

   Right: Barcelona is *a* European football club.

Note: Although 'European' starts with the vowel letter 'E' this letter is pronounced with the consonant sound /j/. Here, sound, rather than letter, counts. For more, see the section on indefinite articles.

4. **Wrong**: There are *much* students in the lecture hall.

   Right: There are *many* students in the lecture hall.

5. **Wrong**: The worshippers are going to *the* church.

   Right: The worshippers are going to church.

Note: When you talk about attending church as a worshipper, school as a student or hospital as a patient, do not use the definite article 'the'.

6. **Wrong**: A friend of mine lives in United Kingdom.

   Right: A friend of mine lives in *the* United Kingdom.

Note: Unique nouns such as United Kingdom, United States of America, etc should be introduced by the definite article 'the' when we talk about them. Likewise, their abbreviations should be preceded by 'the' as in: 'A friend of mine lives in the UK'. Conversely, when such abbreviations are pronounced as words (pronounceable acronyms), they do not attract 'the' as in:

'Do you like UNESCO's new policy on education?'

7. **Wrong**: The businessman always travels by *a* lorry.

   Right: The businessman always travels by lorry.

Note: If you use 'by' to talk about means of transportation such as: car, train, aeroplane, boat, etc, leave out the indefinite article 'a' or 'an'.

8. **Wrong**: *No any* food is left for you.

   Right: *No* food is left for you.

   Right: *Not any* food is left for you.

Note: Do not combine 'no' with 'any'.

9. **Wrong**: A good teacher would not want *some* of his students to fail.

    Right: A good teacher would not want *any* of his students to fail.

10. **Wrong**: *That your* goat is very stubborn.

    Right: *That* goat of yours is very stubborn.

    Right: *Your* goat is very stubborn.

9.3 Syntactic Errors

These are errors that affect phrases, clauses or sentences which we discussed in Part Two entitled 'Syntax' in this book. Syntactic errors are, therefore, structural errors and they include the following types by Fakuade (2012):

9.3.1 Sentence Logic Error

Clauses and phrases in sentences exist in a logical relationship which should not be broken. One of such relationships occurs when a phrase is used as a modifier in a sentence. Normally, a modifier should be as close as possible to whatever it modifies. When the modifier is placed in an awkward position, it distorts the flow of communication in the sentence, resulting in a sentence logic error as in the following examples:

*If you wash your hands before and after eating *with clean water and soap*, you will be healthier.

The above sentence is illogical because the phrase 'with clean water and soap' is in the wrong place. The phrase should have come after the word 'wash' because it is about what will be used in washing:

If you wash your hands *with clean water and soap* before and after eating, you will be healthier.

*Here is the man who killed the python *with bare hands* which had been terrorizing the community.

In the above example, there is the confusion of thinking that the community was being terrorized by the man's hand. This is because of the wrong positioning of the phrase 'with bare hands'. Below is the correction.

Here is the man who, *with bare hands,* killed the python which had been terrorizing the community.

9.3.2 Faulty Subordination

In a complex sentence which contains a subordinate clause and a main clause, less important information should be in the subordinate clause while more important information is put in the main clause. If this rule is reversed, we have an error of faulty subordination as in:

*Mary Slessor, who stopped the killing of twins in Nigeria, was born in 1848.

Stopping the killing of twins is more important than when Mary Slessor was born. Hence, the former goes into the main clause while the latter goes into the subordinate clause so that we have:

Mary Slessor, who was born in 1848, stopped the killing of twins in Nigeria.

9.3.3 Excessive Subordination

This refers to the error of stringing too many subordinate clauses (adjectival clauses) together in an effort to qualify a number of nouns in a sentence. The result of this is a cumbersome sentence.

*Rita's brother, *who is a medical doctor,* works in a hospital *which is a new hospital* that is located beside the primary school that she attended.

The above sentence contains excessive subordination. One way to solve this is to eliminate the unnecessary subordinate clauses such as 'who is a medical doctor' and 'which is a new hospital' and replace them respectively with an appositive phrase and a noun phrase. This is partly because, as Fakuade (2012, p. 205) pointed out, it is 'better to use an appositive phrase for a subordinate clause that merely identifies a person'.

Rita's brother, *a medical doctor*, works in *a new hospital* located beside the primary school that she attended.

Another way of doing this is by splitting the long sentence into two thus:

Rita's brother is a medical doctor. He works in a new hospital located beside the primary school that she attended.

9.3.4 Faulty Parallelism

A sentence containing a series of ideas in the same grammatical pattern is said to be parallel. That is, the sentence contains a series of nouns or adjectives or phrases or clauses, etc.

Series of gerunds: She likes swimming and running.

Series of adjectives: The men are armed, powerful, and dangerous.

Series of noun clauses: Confess to the police everything about the riot: how it started, why it started, when it started and what your role was.

However, when two or more different grammatical patterns are indiscriminately combined, faulty parallelism results, as in:

*She likes swimming and to run. (A gerund and an infinitive)

*The men are armed, powerful and they can kill. (Two adjectives and one clause)

*Confess to the police everything about the riot: how it started, why it started, when it started and your role in it. (Three clauses and one phrase)

9.3.5 Concord Error

Lack of agreement between the various parts of a sentence is also a syntactic error. We have discussed 'Concord in English' elaborately as a sub-topic in Chapter Seven and you may wish to refer to it for more on concord errors. There are different types of concord error. Let us examine this example of subject-verb concord error:

*A *number* (S) of illegal buildings *was* (V) demolished by the government.

Some people tend to think that 'number' is the subject of the sentence and they would use 'was' (a singular verb), as in the wrong example above. The expression 'A number of illegal' in the sentence is only a pre-modifier to the noun 'buildings' which is the subject of the sentence. Therefore, since 'buildings' is plural, a plural verb should be used thus:

A number of illegal *buildings* (S) *were* (V) demolished by the government.

9.3.6 Vague Pronoun Reference

Pronouns normally make reference to their antecedents and so, every pronoun should have a clear antecedent. Without a clear antecedent, the reference becomes vague and this leads to ambiguity as shown by the following sentence:

*The woman beat her daughter because *she* was drunk.

This is vague because we do not know who the pronoun 'she' refers to (the woman or her daughter?). Hence, we do not know who was drunk. To disambiguate the sentence, we can say:

The drunk woman beat her daughter. OR

The woman beat her drunk daughter.

9.3.7 Dangling Modifiers

In noun phrases, nouns usually have pre-modifiers and/or post-modifiers as we have in 'all the four children of the lawyer' where 'all the four' is the pre-modifier, 'children' is the head of the noun phrase and 'of the lawyer' is the post-modifier. There is a dangling modifier when a modifier has nothing to modify in a sentence because the head is not clearly stated. In other words, a dangling modifier has no referent. A dangling modifier can be a verbal element, a prepositional phrase or an elliptical clause. It is common with passive structures and it can be at the beginning or at the end of a sentence. An example is:

**Moving round Dubai*, a lot of beautiful places were seen.

The verbal structure 'Moving round Dubai' is a dangling modifier because we do not know whom it refers to i.e. who was moving. Fakuade (2012, p. 217) recommended two solutions to dangling modifiers:

1. Restructuring the sentence so that the modifier is clearly attached to the right word:

    Moving round Dubai, we saw a lot of beautiful places.

2. Expanding the dangler into a full subordinate clause:

    When we moved round Dubai, we saw a lot of beautiful places.

When a farmer, my father used to cultivate food crops.

The elliptical clause 'When a farmer' in the sentence above is a dangling modifier because it has no referent. Correction:

When my father was a farmer, he used to cultivate food crops.

9.3.8 Sentence Fragments

Unlike 'fragmentary sentences', a type of minor sentences discussed in Chapter Seven, sentence fragments are parts of sentences written as complete sentences which are incomprehensible within their context of use. There is a sentence fragment because the structure in question lacks an element that is required to make it a complete sentence. The missing element may be the subject, the predicate or an independent clause, as in:

*Whereas she was to blame. (Independent clause missing)

*Two of the people who attended the wedding. (Predicate missing)

The first erroneous structure above is a dependent clause and needs an independent clause to make it complete while the second one is a phrase which lacks a predicate. Below is a revision of the sentences:

She blamed me whereas she was to blame.

Two of the people who attended the wedding lost their phones.

Note that sentence fragments are different from minor sentences which are usually comprehensible in their context of use.

9.3.9 Run-on Sentences and Comma Splices

There is a run-on sentence when two separate sentences are written together as one without a proper punctuation mark or a conjunction.

*I don't have the money now we've not been paid.

If a comma is used to separate the sentences, then another related error, known as 'comma splice', results (Greenbaum & Nelson, 2009, p. 208), as in:

*I don't have the money now, we've not been paid.

There are several possible ways in which these errors can be corrected. The long sentence could be separated into an independent clause and a dependent clause; it could be divided into two independent clauses separated with a semi-colon and it could be divided into two separate sentences with each sentence ending in a full stop.

I don't have the money now because we've not been paid.

I don't have the money now; we've not been paid.

I don't have the money now. We've not been paid.

9.3.10 Inconsistent Tenses

This refers to the use of the present tense when the past tense should be used and vice versa. It normally happens in sentences containing two or more clauses. Normally, all the clauses in a sentence should be in the same tense. Indiscriminate use of different tenses in the same sentence leads to the error of inconsistent tenses. This error relates to 'Sequence of Tenses' which has been explained in Chapter Three of this book. For emphasis, let us see one example of this.

*They have *eaten* their food and *drank* their water.

The first clause is in perfect tense (eaten) while the second one is in past tense (drank). This is inconsistent and wrong. To correct this, the same tenses must be used in both clauses thus:

They *ate* their food and *drank* their water. (Both past tenses) OR

They have *eaten* their food and *drunk* their water. (Both perfect tenses)

There are other types of syntactic error which time and space will not permit us to discuss. We have, therefore, selected the above common types for the purpose of illustration.

Revision Exercise 17

A. Identify the errors in these sentences and rewrite the sentences correctly.

1. Listen, I have an information for you all.
2. Rose had to change her stained beddings immediately.
3. You are cordially invited to my send-forth programme.
4. The billionaire has bought a luxurious bus for his church.
5. Indisciplined people hardly succeed in life.
6. Our school is more better than yours.
7. My sister is an alumnus of University of Nigeria, Nsukka.
8. The prize does not worth the trouble.
9. I'm happy because I'm understanding the lecture.
10. I have been here since one hour now.
11. They have promised to pay the debt instalmentally.
12. Though she was ill but she finished the food.
13. Between Femi and I, who is the tallest?
14. Both the boss and them are to blame for the disaster.
15. A number of the workers has been reinstated.
16. The boy as well as the girl were busy with homework.

17. Emmanuel is an expert in swimming.
18. The contestants comprise of eight men and two women.
19. Gofwen has just arrived from United States of America.
20. There is no any money in the bank.

B. List and explain any five types of syntactic errors that you have read about and give an example of each type.

Chapter Ten

APPENDIX: THE MECHANICS OF WRITING

In this section, we shall discuss the mechanics of capitalization, punctuation and spelling which are essential for good writing. Note that most of what we shall discuss in this chapter is from Dada (2020).

10.1 Capitalization

This aspect deals with the use of capital letters. The English alphabet has 26 letters and each letter has both a capital and a small form. The first three capital letters are: A, B, C, while their small correspondents are: a, b, c. The letters are not used haphazardly or indiscriminately. Capital letters are used for:

a. the first letter of every sentence:

Dogs are domestic animals. Are you hungry?

b. the pronoun 'I' irrespective of its position in a sentence:

Gbenga, Kunle, you and I are friends.

c. the first letter of the first and the last words and all the open-class words in the titles of publications (books, articles, etc) e.g. *Half of a Yellow Sun, The Tribune*, etc.

d. proper nouns: specific names of persons, places, animals, organizations, days of the week, months of the year, festivals, bodies of water, mountains, languages, etc. (See the section on 'proper nouns' in Chapter Three for examples of these nouns.)
e. titles attached to proper nouns or used in place of proper nouns, without an adjective or determiner, as in: Are you Dr Nelson? I saw Pastor here a while ago.
f. kinship terms or words of family relationship e.g. son, sister, father, aunt, etc used without an adjective or determiner e.g. I told only Mother about it because Father was not around.
g. for the word 'Sir' or 'Madam' in the salutations of formal letters.

10.2 Punctuation

Punctuation is the use of signs or marks to divide our sentences meaningfully in writing. The signs that are used are therefore called 'punctuation marks'. Consider the use of punctuation marks in these two sentences and the meanings derived from them:

1. A woman, without her man, is nothing.
2. A woman: without her, man is nothing!

The first sentence shows the importance of a man to a woman while the second sentence shows the importance of a woman to a man. The following are the common punctuation marks and their uses. The punctuation marks are enclosed in brackets ( ) which are also a punctuation mark.

1. **The full stop** (BrE) or **period** (AmE) (.) is used:

a. to mark the end of a declarative sentence or a statement e.g.

   Thunder struck. There was lightening. Rain fell heavily.

b. sometimes in abbreviations e.g.

   Aug., Oct., e.g., Prof., N.G.O., P.T.O., P.H.C.N., etc.

   Note that the full stop is not necessary if the final letter of a word ends the abbreviation e.g. Mr, Dr, Lt, etc and not necessary in long established abbreviations e.g. AU, UN, WAEC, etc.

   Note that abbreviations are usually written in modern British English without full stops while the use of full stops in abbreviations in American English is normal (Swan, 2005, p. 2).

c. in internet and email addresses e.g. www.unilorin.edu.ng

2. **The comma** (,) is generally used to mark short pauses in writing such as:

   a. to separate items in a list e.g.

   I need bread, milk, Bournvita and honey.

   Buy me salt, pepper, tomatoes and okra.

   b. to separate phrases or clauses e.g.

   If you work hard, attend lectures regularly, obey instructions and pray to God, you will succeed in your studies.

   c. before and after a phrase or clause that gives extra information e.g.

Chief Bolarin, our school principal, was a no-nonsense man.

d. to separate an introductory expression such as a transitional marker from the rest of the sentence e.g.

In conclusion, honesty pays.

Before long, he had become used to the weather.

e. to separate a question tag from the rest of the sentence e.g.

I am eating, aren't I?

The woman is not your mother, is she?

f. before a short quotation e.g.

The president said, 'We are out of the recession'.

Note that the comma is generally not necessary where a coordinating conjunction such as *and, but, or* is used because not using it does not constitute any difficulty to meaning.

3. **The question mark** (?) is used:

a. as the name suggests, to ask a direct question e.g.

How old are you? Did he come late?

b. before a date, to express doubt:

Shakespeare was born in ?1616. (Unsure of the date.)

4. **The exclamation mark** (BrE) or **exclamation point** (AmE) (!) is used:

a. at the end of a word or sentence that expresses strong emotion e.g.

That's great! Wow!

b. in informal written English, you can use more than one exclamation mark or an exclamation mark and a question mark (Hornby, 2010, p. R23) e.g.

Doctor: Your wife has just been delivered of a set of sextuplets.

Mr Sam: Sextu what!?

5. **The apostrophe** (') is used:
   a. with letter 's' to show ownership e.g. Mary's dress (sg), my brother's car (sg), ladies' bags (pl), men's shoes (pl), farmers' children (pl), Agnes' or Agnes's money (sg), Jesus' name (sg), Ade's and Ola's bicycles (individual ownership), Ade and Ola's bicycle (joint ownership).

   Note that where two /s/ sounds already appear in a word, only the apostrophe should be used, as in: Jesus' name, Moses' rod, etc.

   b. to show contraction or omission of a letter(s) or figure(s) e.g.

   it's (it is), I'm (I am), He was born in '75 (1975).

   Note that 'its' (a determiner) is not hyphenated and that 'am' is not the short form of 'I am'.

   c. with 's' to form the plural of a letter or number e.g.

   Cross you t's and dot your i's. He lived in the US in the 1980's.

6. **The hyphen** (-) is used:
   a. to form a compound word from two or more words e.g. father-in-law, well-written, Afro-British, face-to-face, etc.

b. to write compound numbers e.g. forty-one, twenty-six, etc.

c. sometimes to separate a prefix ending in a vowel from a word starting with the same vowel e.g. co-operate, pre-eminent and so on.

d. to divide a word between two lines e.g. mis-takes (where 'mis', ends a line and 'takes' begins another). Words can be so divided morphologically (style in BrE) e.g. teach-er or syllabically (style in AmE) e.g. tea-cher

7. **The inverted commas/quotation marks** (' ') or (" ") are used:

   a. to enclose expressions and punctuation marks in direct speech e.g.

   'Stop there!' he ordered.

   b. around expressions that are unusual for the context or technical expressions e.g.

   The pastor was helped by 'area boys'.

   c. to enclose titles of publications (books, newspapers, novels, etc.)

   Chinua Achebe wrote 'There Was a Country'.

   d. around short quotations or sayings e.g.

   According to Disreali, 'Little things affect little minds.'

   Note that while single quotation marks are used in British English, the double style is preferred in American English (Hornby, 2010, p. R23).

8. **The colon** (:) is used:

a. to introduce a list of items e.g.

   Get me the following from the UK: a phone, jewellery and perfume.

b. to introduce a long, indented quotation e.g. Halliday (2004) submitted that: ...

c. in formal writing, before a phrase or clause that gives additional information about the main clause. Here, you can also use a semicolon or a full stop but not a comma.

   Thunder struck: the goats ran helter-skelter.

9. **The semicolon** (;) is used:

   a. in place of a comma, to separate parts of a sentence that already have commas e.g.

   The meeting was attended by the Vice Chancellor, University of Ibadan; the Vice Chancellor, University of Lagos; the Vice Chancellor, University of Ilorin and the Vice Chancellor, University of Jos.

   b. in formal writing, to separate two main clauses that are not joined by a conjunction.

   The clouds have gathered; it will soon rain.

10. **The dash** (–) is used:

    a. in informal written English, instead of a colon or semicolon, to show that what follows is a summary or conclusion of what precedes it e.g.

    Children were jumping, mothers were singing, fathers were clapping – it was a great celebration.

    b. singly or in pairs, to mark off an afterthought from the rest of the sentence e.g.

The choir sang – I mean, impressively – at the concert.

11. **The ellipsis/dots** (…) are used:

    a. to show that a word or words have been omitted from a piece of writing e.g.

    That species … stronger than this. (is, are)

Note that the dots are only three. There will be four only where the ellipsis ends a sentence, in which case the full stop is the fourth dot. Even in this case, the dots and the full stop should be separated with a space.

12. **The slash/oblique** (/) is used:

    a. to separate alternative words or phrases e.g. male/female, single/married

    b. in internet and email addresses, to separate the various parts e.g.

    https://www.halliday.com/functionalgrammar

13. **The brackets** (BrE) or **parentheses** (AmE) ( ) are used:

    a. to separate extra information or a comment from the rest of an expression e.g.

    Bishop David Oyedepo (founder of Living Faith Church) is a billionaire.

    b. to enclose numbers or letters in texts e.g.

    Our objectives are: (1) to increase output (2) to improve quality and (3) to maximize profits.

    c. around cross-references e.g.

    Chomsky's earlier work on Transformation Generative Grammar (see page 10) suggested that …

14. **The square brackets** (BrE) or **brackets** (AmE) [ ] are used:
    a. to enclose words inserted to make a quotation grammatically correct e.g.
       'The house [has] been completed.'
    b. with 'sic' to show that a quotation is grammatically wrong e.g.
       'The house have [sic] been completed.'
15. **The caret** (˄) is placed below a text to show omission e.g.
    Stop ˄ a noise. (where 'making' has been omitted)

10.3 Spelling

It is important that words are correctly spelt. This is because every error of spelling, just like the other mechanics, is penalized. Adegbite (2012), cited in Dada (2020), gave the following causes of spelling errors and guides on correct spelling.

A. Causes/Sources of Wrong Spellings

1. Wrong association of spelling with pronunciation

Wrong	Correct
comitee	committee
campain	campaign
govment	government
jelos	jealous
litrature	literature
acomodation	accommodation
playright	playwright
colum	column

seprate   separate
exitement   excitement

2. Confusion caused by homophones or words that sound alike: flower/flour, buy/bye, check/cheque, fair/fare, fowl/foul, hair/hare, mail/male, morning/mourning, pray/prey, sight/site, tale/tail, etc.

3. Wrong spelling due to minimal pairs and poor pronunciation: bath/birth, fear/fare, hear/heir, seat/sit, taught/thought, walk/work, there/their, ceased/seized, order/other, quiet/quite, etc.

4. Confusion of words that have the letters 'ie' or 'ei': 'ie' in believe, relieve, thief, chief, sieve but 'ei' in receive, deceive, perceive, ceiling, receipt, seize, etc.

   Note that with the exception of 'sieve', all other words with the sound /s/ among those above, are spelt 'ei'.

5. Unnecessary duplication of letters

Wrong	Correct
writting	writing
occassion	occasion
emmigration	emigration
ommission	omission
proffession	profession
preceed	precede
offerred	offered
refferred	referred

6. Writing of compound words as separate words

Wrong	Correct
home work	homework

class room	classroom
eye sore	eyesore
house fly	housefly
motor cycle	motorcycle
straight forward	straightforward
every thing	everything
some one	someone
no body	nobody
any where	anywhere
never the less	nevertheless
shop keeper	shopkeeper

7. Unnecessary insertion of letters

Wrong	Correct
priviledge	privilege
fourty	forty
pronounciation	pronunciation
interprete	interpret
arguement	argument
truely	truly
nineth	ninth

B. Rules/Guides on Correct Spelling

The following spelling rules will be helpful but care should be taken not to overgeneralize them where they are not applicable.

1. Consonants after short vowel sounds usually spell double especially in suffixes like -ar, -ed -ary, -er, -en, -ing, etc. Examples are:

   a. Double consonants before '-ed' e.g. fitted, wrapped, banned, summed, submitted, committed, mobbed,

skipped, sobbed, ragged, skinned, worshipped, travelled, etc.
   b. Double consonants before '-er' e.g. banner, manner, hotter, robber, potter, runner, seller, worshipper, wrapper, traveller, etc.
   c. Double consonants before '-ing' e.g. banning, begging, cutting, fitting, forgetting, worshipping, lagging, running, sitting, travelling etc.

However, note that single 'l' is acceptable in American English in 'traveled', 'traveler' and 'traveling'.

2. Consonants after long vowel sounds spell single before suffixes like -ing, -er, -ed, etc.
   a. Single consonants after the /a:/ sound e.g. barked, farmer, marking, parting, etc.
   b. Single consonants after the /i:/ sound e.g. cleaning, cleaner, reading, reader, reaping, reaper, etc.
   c. Single consonants after the /u:/ sound e.g. assuming, pruning, pruned, fuming, tuning, tuned, etc.
   d. Single consonants after the /ɔ:/ sound e.g. morning, mourning, sorted, talking, etc.

3. Likewise, consonants after double vowel sounds, technically called diphthongs, are usually single.
   a. Single consonants after the /ai/ sound e.g. citing, cited, fighting, fighter, riding, siting, sited, writing, writer, etc.
   b. Single consonants after the /əu/ sound e.g. coping, coped, hoping, hoped, sewing, sowing, sowed, etc.

c. Single consonants after the /ei/ sound e.g. gaping, gaped, waiting, waiter, waited, duplicating, etc.

4. The letter 't' changes to 's' before the suffix '-ion'.

    admit + ion =   admission
    omit + ion =   omission
    submit + ion =   submission
    commit + ion =   commission
    permit + ion =   permission

Exceptions to this rule include protection, eruption, election, selection, correction, etc.

5. Likewise, one 'l' is dropped in 'full' when it is added to a word.

    hope + full =   hopeful
    cheer + full =   cheerful
    mind + full =   mindful
    care + full =   careful
    skill + full =   skilful
    use + full =   useful

C. British Spelling Versus American Spelling

British English and American English are the two standard varieties of the English language but care must be taken not to mix them up while writing. Be consistent in your use of either variety.

British Spelling	American Spelling
axe	ax
centre	center

colour	color
honour	honor
theatre	theater
programme	program
traveller	traveler
sulphur	sulfur
fulfil	fulfill
(have) got	(have) gotten

Always consult a good dictionary whenever you are not sure of the spelling of a word.

Revision Exercise 18

The passage below contains errors of capitalization, punctuation and spelling. Rewrite it, correcting all the errors.

tommorrow is friday and its going to be a very busy day for me i have to wake up as early as 5am to pray and begin the house chores when i finish them i will brush my teeth bath eat and go to davids house david and i have been freinds since childhood both of us attended royal academy abuja and kings collcgc lagos tommorrow is his uncles birthday and weve planned to attend the party together the man was born on the 25th december 1970 which means he was born on a christmas day can you calculate what age he will be marking uncle gbade popularly known as dr gbade is a medical doctor who resides in atlanta in the united states of america however he has decided to come and celebrate the birthday with family and friends in nigeria david told me their will be lots of food and drinks at the party uncle gbade hopes to return to the usa on the 8th of january exactly a weak after new years day every body likes uncle gbade because he is generous and jovial after the busy days activities hopefully i will get back home in the evening full but tired and quitely retire to bed

REFERENCES

Adedimeji, M.A. & Alabi, T.A. (2003). Basic elements of English language grammar. In O. Obafemi & S. Babatunde (Eds) *Studies and discourse in English language* (pp. 28 – 59). Ilorin: Haytee Press and Publishing Company Nigeria Ltd.

Adegbija, E. (1998). A review of basic English grammar. In E. Adegbija (Ed.) *Effective communication in higher education: The use of English* (pp. 113-139). Ilorin: Unilorin Press.

Adichie, C.N. (2006). *Half of a yellow sun.* Lagos: Farafina.

Afolayan, A. (1977). The surface and deep planes of grammar in the systemic model. In S.H.O. Tomori's *The morphology and syntax of present-day English: An introduction* (pp. 111-132). Ibadan: Heinemann.

Akmajian A., Demers R.A., Farmer A.K. & Harnish R.M. (2010). *Linguistics: An introduction to language and communication.* New Delhi: PHI Learning Private Limited.

Aremo, B. (2010). *An introduction to English sentences.* Ibadan: SCRIBO Publications.

Babatunde, S. (2003). The grammatical patterns of English. In O. Obafemi & S. Babatunde (Eds) *Studies and discourse in English language* (pp.101-120). Ilorin: Haytee Press and Publishing Company Nigeria Ltd.

Banjo, A. (1996). *Making a virtue of necessity: An overview of the English language in Nigeria.* Ibadan: Ibadan University Press.

Crystal, D. (2015). *A dictionary of linguistics and phonetics (sixth edition).* U.S.A: Blackwell Publishing.

Dada, G.O. (2016). The structure of English sentences: An eclectic approach. In S. Ore-Oluwa (Ed.) *Issues in linguistics and literary studies* (pp. 1-12). Jos: AIS Publishing Ltd.

Dada, G.O. (2017). English modal auxiliary verbs as stylistic variants. In J.C. Ukazu et al (Eds.) *Readings in languages* (pp. 69-75). Pankshin, Plateau State: Obedtor Press (Nig) Ltd.

Dada. G.O. (2020). Basic English composition. In D. Rinji. R. Gowon, M. Adedimeji, O. Odewumi, A. Chuwang & P. Longdet (Eds) Studies in English education for undergraduates (Pp. 64-89). Jos: BALOZ Design Studio Ltd.

Duntoye, J.A. (1996) Grammar. In J.A. Duntoye (Ed). *Language and communication skills* (pp. 149-173). Ilorin: The

English Language Department, Kwara State College of Education, Ilorin.

Egbe, D.I. (2005). *An explanatory transformational generative grammar of English.* Lagos, Nigeria: Ededuan Publishing Co. Ltd.

Eyisi, J. (2015). *Common errors in the use of English.* Onitsha, Nigeria: Africana First Publishers Plc.

Fakuade, G. (2012). *English grammar for schools and colleges.* Ilorin, Nigeria: Haytee Press and Publishing Nig. Ltd.

Greenbaum, S. & Nelson, G. (2009). *An introduction to English grammar.* Great Britain: Pearson Education limited.

Halliday, M.A.K. & Matthiessen, C.M.I.M. (2014) *Halliday's introduction to functional grammar.* Oxon: Routledge.

Hornby, A.S. (2015). *Oxford advanced learner's dictionary of current English.* United Kingdom: Oxford University Press.

Jackson, H. (2002). *Grammar and vocabulary: A resource book for students.* London: Routledge.

Jowitt, D. & Nnamonu, S. (1985). *Common errors in English.* England: Longman.

Jowitt, D. (1991). *Nigerian English usage: An introduction.* Lagos: Longman Nigeria Plc.

Kieffer, J.M. & Lesaux, N.K. (2007). Breaking down words to build meaning: Morphology, vocabulary and reading comprehension in the urban classroom. In R.B. Cooter & J.H. Perkins (Eds), *The Reading Teacher: A Journal of Research-Based Classroom Practice* (pp. 134-144). USA: International Reading Association.

Lamidi, M.T. (2016). *Aspects of Chomskyan grammar.* Ibadan: University Press Plc.

Leech, G. & Svartvik, J. (2012). *A communicative grammar of English.* India: Pearson.

Lyons, J. (1981). *Language and linguistics: An introduction.* United Kingdom: Cambridge University Press.

Medubi, O. (2007). A history of the English language. In O. Obafemi, G.A. Ajadi & V.A. Alabi (Eds.) *Critical perspectives on English language and Literature* (pp. 1-13). Ilorin: The Department of English, University of Ilorin.

Murthy, J.D. (2012). *Contemporary English grammar.* Lagos: Book Master.

Odebunmi, A. (2006). *Meaning in English: An introduction.* Ogbomoso, Nigeria: Critical Sphere.

Odebunmi, A. (2016). Language, context and society: A theoretical anchorage. In A. Odebunmi & K.A. Ayoola (Eds) *Language, context and society: A festschrift for Wale Adegbite*. Ile-Ife, Nigeria: Obafemi Awolowo University Press.

Ojo, J.O. (2011). *A contemporary functional grammar of English*. Ago-Iwoye, Ogun State: Olabisi Onabanjo University Press.

Olujide, M.T. (1999). An overview of English syntax. In E. Adegbija (Ed) *The English language and literature in English: An introductory handbook* (pp. 46-69). Ilorin: The Department of Modern European Languages, University of Ilorin.

Osisanwo, W. (2002). *An introductory analytical grammar of English for undergraduates*. Lagos: Femolus-Fetop Publishers.

Quirk, R. & Greenbaum, S. (1973). *A university grammar of English*. India: Pearson Education Pte. Ltd.

Sood, M (n.d.). *Comprehensive English grammar*. New Delhi: Goodwill Publishing House.

Soyinka, W. (1985). *The man died*. Ibadan: Spectrum Books Limited.

Strumpf, M. & Douglas, A. (n.d.). *The complete grammar.* New Delhi, India: Goodwill Publishing House.

Swan, M. (2005). *Practical English usage.* Oxford: Oxford University Press.

Tomori, S.H.O. (1977). *The morphology and syntax of present-day English: An introduction.* London: Heinemann.

Udaa, J.I.; Ohiemi, J. & Tyohemba, T. (2016). A contemporary approach to defining parts of speech. In O. Ayodabo; U.N., Butari & O.A. Solomon (Eds) *Linguistics, language and literature.* Lokoja: Department of English and Literary studies, Federal University, Lokoja.

Whitebread, R.M. & Ajayi, D. (2012). *Lexis and structure: A guide to the SSCE.* Ibadan: Spectrum Books Ltd.

Wren, P.C. & Martin, H. (2010). *High school English grammar and composition.* New Delhi: S. Chand and Company Ltd.

Yule, G. (1996). *The study of language.* United Kingdom: Cambridge University Press.

http://en.m.wikipedia.org/wiki/Plurale-tantum. Retrieved on 12th April, 2018.

https://akademia.com.ng/types-sentences-according-structure-examples (2017). Retrieved on 3rd January, 2019.

https://www.brighthubeducation.com. Retrieved on 1st May, 2019.

kathysteinermann.com/Musings/absolute/. Retrieved on 22nd April, 2020.

languagelinguistics.com/2014/06/19/empty-morphemes-in-linguistics/. Retrieved on 11th March, 2020.

za.pinterest.com/amp/pin/525302744007755519. Retrieved on 10th February, 2019.

www.ingramcontent.com/pod-product-compliance
Lightning Source LLC
Chambersburg PA
CBHW071335080526
44587CB00017B/2850